NEW POEMS

1955

New Poems

1952

1953

1954

New Poems

1955

Edited by

PATRIC DICKINSON

J. C. HALL

ERICA MARX

with an introduction

London

MICHAEL JOSEPH

First published by
MICHAEL JOSEPH LTD
26 Bloomsbury Street
London, W.C.1
1955

Set and printed in Great Britain by Unwin Brothers Ltd., at the
Gresham Press, Woking, in Bembo type, eleven point, leaded, on
paper made by Henry Bruce at Currie, Scotland, and bound by
James Burn at Esher

Contents

INTRODUCTION
[*p.* 7]

THE POEMS
[*p.* 9]

INDEX OF TITLES
AND AUTHORS
[*p.* 115]

THE CONTRIBUTORS
[*p.* 117]

Introduction

THIS is the fourth anthology in the annual P.E.N. series. The general aim of the series is now well known, and all we need do by way of introduction is to point out how our anthology differs significantly from those of our predecessors.

In the first place, the P.E.N. made it a rule on this occasion that no poet should send us more than three poems for consideration. There were good reasons for this. The entry, hitherto unrestricted, had increased astonishingly with each volume, and when the editors of the 1954 anthology were faced with no less than ten thousand poems it was clear that in future some restriction would have to be made. This, of course, involved the risk that poets might not make the happiest choice from their work when deciding which three poems to submit. In the outcome we do not feel that this risk was unreasonable. It is possible that, with an unrestricted entry, a few poets might have been more fully represented in these pages; but we are far from convinced that the book as a whole would have been substantially larger.

The second distinctive feature of our anthology is its mode of presentation. As a glance will show, the poems are printed anonymously. This method is not, of course, original. But this is the first time, as far as we know, that it has been used for an anthology of contemporary verse. Our intention has been deliberately to shift the emphasis from poet to poem, from reputation to actual achievement, and so to encourage the reader to work for his opinions. In return we ask the reader to co-operate by not referring to the index at the end until he has given the poems his fair attention. We hope that this will prove stimulating even to those who recognize some of these poems from their previous appearance elsewhere.

A word must also be said about the order in which the poems are arranged. After some thought we decided against an automatic order (such as alphabetically by first lines) in favour of a more tentative, and we hope more interesting, arrangement. As far as possible we have tried to arrange the poems so that, read consecutively, they speak to each other, exchanging confidences and ideas, occasionally answering each other back. With anything as individual as a poem (and a poem, let us emphasize, chosen wholly on its individual merit), such a scheme can only be rough and ready. If our arrangement adds to the reader's enjoyment, so much the better. If not, he may still have the pleasure of supplying for himself correspondences which we missed.

Finally, it may be asked what criteria guided us in making our selections. All we can say is that we looked for poems which seemed to us genuine and alive, with some positive quality of poetic interest. We saw no virtue in being representative merely for its own sake, and fashionable 'schools,' as such, did not concern us. If any poet of reputation is missed from these pages, the reason more often than not is that he failed to send us anything for consideration—a handicap we might have overcome by soliciting, had not soliciting seemed to us out of place now that these anthologies are well known. In the end we asked for about half a dozen poems which we had seen and admired elsewhere.

Out of some five thousand poems submitted to us we have chosen sixty-four. This may seem an uncharitably small proportion. But perhaps, after all, it is as generous a harvest as one can reasonably expect in any one year of poetry.

THE EDITORS

Acknowledgements are due to the B.B.C., *Encounter*, *Fishing Gazette*, *The Irish Times*, *Lines Review*, *The Listener*, *The London Magazine*, *The New Statesman and Nation*, *The Observer*, *Poetry and Poverty*, *The Poetry Review*, *Punch*, *The Saltire Review*, *The Spectator*, *Stand*, *The Times Literary Supplement*.

HOW TO FILL IN A CROSSWORD PUZZLE

FIRST adjust your spectacles and take your pen,
(A pencil will serve equally well) and pick the easiest
   clue:
Here you are: five letters down—'What is Man?'
Clown, Rogue, Beast, or even Saint would do.

Now let's try another going across. Here is one
Which seems more likely than the rest: 'Lethal but Sweet,'
A six-letter word, the first of which is B
If Beast were right for man—the beast with two feet.

Think hard—'Lethal but Sweet.' Assuming Beast is correct,
Breast might fit, the sweet but bladed breast
Of her you hugged, who bled you white and stabbed
To death your groping heart most treacherously.

If, as may well be, you have mistakenly put Beast
Adjustments are required unless you are going to let
This chequered puzzle stay unsolved. Try Rogue instead of
   Beast,
Then 'Lethal but Sweet,' could reasonably be Regret.

Of course the word Clown would fit the first clue you
   attempted
(Yes, I admit this puzzle is confusing)
Then your six-letter word going across might be
Coitus, Create, Cringe, or possibly Crying.

The other word, less likely I suppose, is Saint.
Here the thing 'Lethal but Sweet' would begin with S.
Sinful it might be, Senses or simply Seduce.
The snag about these clues is the alternatives are endless.

Write in the words faintly because you may have to alter
  them,
And be warned. When the puzzle is solved, and like a
  satisfied lover
You lean back sighing and sleepy, then you will find
That the black squares hide the secrets you will never
  uncover.

ILLUSION

THE other train is moving, not our own.
  We sit bewildered, staring through the glass
At windows passing in an endless train,
Crowded with faces we have never known.
In time, perhaps, these carriages will pass
Shocking us to stillness once again.
Yet even now, if we but turn our eyes
Towards the far window, where the voices call,
We see the station still and realize
We are at home, we have not moved at all.

III

THE HOUSE WHERE I WAS BORN

An elegant, shabby, whitewashed house
With a slate roof. Two rows
Of tall sash-windows. Below the porch, at the foot of
The steps, my father, posed
In his pony trap and round clerical hat.
This is all the photograph shows.

No one is left alive to tell me
In which of those rooms I was born,
Or what my mother could see, looking out one April
Morning, her agony done,
Or if there were pigeons to answer my cooings
From that tree to the left of the lawn.

Eloquent house, how well you speak
For him who fathered me there,
With your sanguine face, your moody provincial charm,
And that Anglo-Irish air
Of living beyond one's means to keep up
An era beyond repair.

Reticent house in the far Queen's County,
How much you leave unsaid.
Not a ghost of a hint appears at your placid windows
That she, so youthfully wed,
Who bore me, would move elsewhere very soon
And then, in four years, be dead.

I know that we left you before my seedling
Memory could root and twine
Within you. Perhaps that is why so often I gaze
At your picture and try to divine
Through it the buried treasure, the lost life—
Reclaim what was yours, and mine.

I put up the curtains for them again
And light a fire in their grate:
I bring the young father and mother to lean above me,
Ignorant, loving, complete:
I ask the questions I never could ask them
Until it was too late.

IV

THE CARPENTER

WITH a jack plane in his hands
    My father the carpenter
Massaged the wafering wood,
Making it white and true.

He was skilful with his saws,
Handsaw, bowsaw, hacksaw,
And ripsaw with fishes' teeth
That chewed a plank in a second.

He was fond of silver bits,
The twist and countersink—
And the auger in its pit
Chucking shavings over its shoulder.

I remember my father's hands,
For they were supple and strong
With fingers that were lovers—
Sensuous strokers of wood:

He fondled the oak, the strong-man
Who holds above his head
A record-breaking lift
Of thick commingled boughs;

And he touched with his finger-tips
Dark boards of elm and alder,
Spruce, and cherry for lathes
That turned all days to spring.

My father's hands were tender
Upon my tender head,
But they were massive on massive
Beam for building a house,

And delicate on the box wood
Leaning against the wall
As though placed there in a corner
For a moment and then forgotten,

And expert as they decoded
Archives unlocked by the axe—
The pretty medullary rays
Once jammed with a traffic of food

To a watched and desired tree
That he marked and felled in the winter,
The tracks of tractors smashing
The ground where violets grew,

Then bound in chains and dragged
To the slaughtering circular saw:
A railway dulcimer
Rang the passing bell

Of my father's loved ones,
Though there was no grief in him
Caressing the slim wood, hearing
A robin's piccolo song.

V

JESUS AND HIS MOTHER

My only son, more God's than mine,
Stay in this garden ripe with pears.
The yielding of their substance wears
A modest and contented shine:
And when they weep with age, not brine
But lazy syrup are their tears.
'I am my own and not my own.'

He seemed much like another man,
That silent foreigner who trod
Outside my door with lily rod:
How could I know what I began
Meeting the eyes more furious than
The eyes of Joseph, those of God?
I was my own and not my own.

And who are these twelve labouring men?
I do not understand your words:
I taught you speech, we named the birds,
You marked their big migrations then
Like any child. So turn again
To silence from the place of crowds.
'I am my own and not my own.'

Why are you sullen when I speak?
Here are your tools, the saw and knife
And hammer on your bench. Your life
Is measured here in week and week
Planed as the furniture you make,
And I will teach you like a wife
To be my own and all my own.

Who like an arrogant wind blown
Where he may please, needs no content?
Yet I remember how you went
To speak with scholars in furred gown.
I hear an outcry in the town;
Who carries that dark instrument?
'One all his own and not his own.'

Treading the green and nimble sward,
I stare at a strange shadow thrown.
Are you the boy I bore alone,
No doctor near to cut the cord?
I cannot reach to call you Lord,
Answer me as my only son.
'I am my own and not my own.'

VI

ADOPTED CHILD

SHE was twelve when other children told her.
Till then, she had loved, as children do
without question, the man and woman
who now were not her father and her mother.

Afterwards, she loved them consciously
for their conscious love, and she became
more filial and devoted than a child
loving by nature; whilst that natural love
ranged through imagined cities for a man
and woman she need not forgive.

Now, as a woman, hearing the village talk,
'The mother's sin's repeated in the child,'
her eyes are bright, for in her sleep
there walks a longing for unguarded love.

THE SHAPE OF A BIRD

'BREAK off your argument,
Dearest of patient friends with whom
I have turned this muted wood
To a long, carpeted room,
Hearing you always invent
New cures for a sickly mood.
Drop your eyes to the floor:
We have strolled, you see, by accident
To a corner we missed before—
What do you see with your
Imaginative eye?'

'Feathers—a circle of grey:
Little arena empty of strife:
Some murdered ring-dove.   Why?—
Very well!   I see the way
Death is haunted by life:
A circle of feathers keeping
Vaguely the shape of a bird;
Though, at mere thought of a wind's creeping,
Each could be separately stirred,
The whole image blurred.—
What would you have me see?'

'A man and his children keeping
Vaguely the shape of a family still,
   When the meaning is lost that she
   Alone could give to that word.
   Or again, that man alone,
   Keeping by effort of will
   The shape of the self she freed,
Like the shape of a lost, migratory bird.
   With all coherence gone.
   With moods that one by one
   To the wind's humour succeed.'

A BURIAL

Of one who was much to me,
  Nothing to anyone else,
I shall have least to say,
For silence is not false.
Once when I walked in iron
Through dead formalities,
I wished that I need not summon
The barbarous preaching voice.
So simple an act as death
Needs no pomp to excuse,
Nor any expense of breath
To magnify what is.
The sun shot the red apples,
Flies swung on summer air,
The world swam in green ripples
As a slow sea might stir.
There is no more to do
But to turn and go away,
Turn and finally go
From one who was much to me,
Nothing to anyone else.
Often it must be so
And always words be false.
Child, do you blame what is?
Child, do you blame what was?

AT LENGTHENING RANGE

WAIT for me in that other gift of being,
Where waiting is no word, for Time is out.
Remember, since you died I have been seeing
Things of no brilliance. If I grope in doubt,
Be patient for a while, and let me trace
One outline of what matters, like a face.

Be slow to flash with unpredicted pleasure,
Lovely, impetuous, welcoming one—be slow
Even to remind. Dull, let my dulness treasure
Some instance of contentment long ago,
When the mere drip-drop of the rain could bless.
Point the safe context in lost happiness!

Small need for such a tact when first you died!
I safely could have joined you anywhere:
Turned at a sound, and simply laid aside
Both book and grief, because you waited there.
The days were full of doors through which you
    might
Come back, before the failing of the light. . . .

How bright the land of loss!—inviting, too:
As though the land of having were extended
Through one vast gap of unimagined view
To the world's end, could such a world be ended:—
A sunlit, bruised, and thunder-blotted moor
It seemed mere chance we could not both explore!

And yet, it seemed, we did. A prospect so
Prodigious, full of meaning, and exalted,
Told me you saw, unseen. I felt it grow,
As climbers—on from where they briefly halted—
Feel challenge bud through skylines, dark and vast,
Strangely transforming even the sunlit past.

Oh, that was the early, easy time when you,
Still near, were all but actual among those
Blizzards of loss friends hope to see one through.
(No wind more welcome out of darkness blows.)
All gave the succour, then, grief had not craved . . .
But when you died indeed, they said, 'he's saved.'

And as you died, year to descending year,
Bled out—beyond all skill of heart to stem—
Sweet virtue from the things you cherished here.
I vowed that when it quite deserted them,
Picture or candlestick or glamorous shoes,
New hands should find them, or oblivion lose.

For things receive a glow when love regards them,
A kind of soul, like chattels in a fable,
And keep it, for a while, when love discards them,—
Like a warm necklace on a dressing-table.
But when it cools, no taking-thought can add
To cloth or clay the elated look they had.

Paupered by living on, I trust I may
Yet reach our long-appointed rendezvous
Clutching some icon of our love. But say
Mind cannot last! Oh, if quite void of you,
Quite emptied of your image, wide and blind,
These arms grope forward—be the thing they find!

ORPHEUS

Wild beasts and women sought this man,
  Whose trick of singing could unlock
Their moment for a breathing-space
And let them wander through the clock
In shining brevities of grace.

The dog and harlot both achieved
Their royalties on steps of sound,
Treading a bright imperial air
Above their rank bloodsodden ground.
But as that white, denatured place
Died on them, for the voice was dumb,
Took back into themselves like Kings
Their exiled and appalling slum.

No wonder as the singing man
Grew wholly silent with his tears,
Sealed by gross habitudes of blood
Within their small disfiguring heart,
They sought him in the rattling wood
And tore his lyre strings apart.

Now on a salt unbridled stream
His sacred essence walks abroad
Through cold futurities of dream
in hopeless and Plutonian love.
The clouded animals of sense
Are touched by his grief-stricken eye
And from their blind experience
Follow a vagrant, Orphic cry.

MME. EMILIE TESTE

Voyez-nous, marchant à petits pas, livrés au soleil, aux cyprès, aux cris d'oiseau.—Paul Valéry: Mme. Teste's letter to a friend in *Monsieur Teste.*

IN that ambiguous paradise
Where evening sharpens the cry of birds
You walk with Monsieur Teste. There only
The absent ones, the lovers and lonely,
Seeking or lost wander. Cypresses burn
Dark: a sun wheels in the whitening sky.
He walks with you, the concave man, cold Form
Whom you and the world shall fill yet never
    warm.

Your love, your living flesh, are known
To his starry mathematic. He ordains
That passion deep-sea-dyed shall enter
His crystal awareness, yet the Self at centre
Remain untouched, impersonal.
                    —And you?
Lighting those burial urns or urns of flowers,
You blessedly normal, free among the dead,
Still walk with him and worship whom you
    dread.

XII

THE TALL MAN

THE tall man walks beside me,
    his stride like mine;
      from his cold eyes
I know he will deride me.

The tall man grasps my shoulder,
    his hand is firm;
      he will disturb
my way, he who is older,

stronger, whose will has power
    to shape my need,
      to capture me
anew in every hour.

The tall man has my colour,
    my tilt of head;
      but his the set
eyes of the levered sculler.

Like me feature by feature,
    shape of my shape,
      he has the ways
of a held, purposed creature.

He will invent diversions,
    (my wish like his)
      and he will trick
me on our dark excursions.

26

He will lead me on searches
    into far towns,
    among the crowds
sobbing in suspect churches.

He knows how to discover
    the hidden place
    under the late
lights of the hand-in-glover.

He knows the furthest findings
    of alley ways,
    the narrow gate
of the reversed maze windings.

He knows what oblique pleasure
    will slant my will
    and bend the stiff
paling of my tried measure.

He will devise researches
    to make thought groan,
    for he will show me
the bright, hissing birches.

He will direct my fingers
    to write new words
    for the old curse;
will know where love malingers.

I must take his strange order,
    pay out new coin
    till I am void:
he will allow no hoarder.

The tall man walks beside me,
    his stride like mine;
    from his sharp eyes
I know he will decide me.

XIII

THE WRONG ROAD

THERE was no precise point at which to say
'I am on the wrong road.' So well he knew
Where he wanted to go, he had walked in a dream
Never dreaming he could lose his way.
Besides, for such travellers, it's all but true
That up to a point any road will do
As well as another—so why not walk
Straight on? The trouble is, *after* this point
There's no turning back, not even a fork;
And you never can see that point until
After you have passed it. And when you know
For certain you are lost, there's nothing to do
But go on walking your road, although
You walk in a nightmare now, not a dream.

But are there no danger-signs? Couldn't he see
Something strange about the landscape to show
That he was near where he should not be?
Rather the opposite—perhaps the view
Gave him a too familiar look
And made him feel at home where he had no right
Of way. But when you have gone so far
A landscape says less than it used to do
And nothing seems very strange. He might
Have noticed how, mile after mile, this road
Made easier walking—noticed a lack
Of grit and gradient: *there* was a clue—
Ah yes, if only he'd listened to his feet!
But, as I told you, he walked in a dream.

You can argue it thus or thus:—either the road
Changed gradually under his feet and became
A wrong road, or else it was he who changed
And put the road wrong. We'd hesitate to blame
The traveller for a highway's going askew;
Yet possibly he and it become one
At a certain stage, like means and ends.
For this lost traveller, all depends
On how real the road is to him—not as a mode
Of advancement or exercise—rather, as grain
To timber, intrinsic-real.
                              He can but pursue
His course and believe that, granting the road
Was right at the start, it will see him through
Their errors and turn into the right road again.

XIV

BY HEART

'This gun fires if you drop it; men have died
Unnerved into a careless suicide;
The regulations must not be defied.'

'The regulations lead to suicide;
They drill away until the nerve has died;
This gun fires if you drop it; some have tried.'

THE TRANSPARENT PRISONER

(Broadcast on the eve of the twelfth anniversary of the battle of El Alamein)

THEY took me somewhere sleeping in the desert
Up middle of a minefield near Benghazi:
And I was hungry—but that was later. At first
It was the Germans—you'd hardly call them Nazi—
Polite and battle-hungry happy men
—O I would like to meet those chaps again.

And everything was decent at headquarters,
After we'd picked our way out like with tweezers,
Decent and capable, and we were ordered
Into small companies, and fed or feasted
Better than back in Cairo. So for ten days
We waited, glad in the shade, glad of delays.

Then we were shifted in a desert truck
Back eighty miles, the sun like liquid steel,
The smell of heat, the nagging—until it took
A hard wrench on the memory to dispel
Those green and English places with their sounds
Which hiccuped at me, festering with old wounds.

But it was still the Germans, and one talked
At great length about his home-town, in what
I soon could recognize as Marburg—talked
And was glad of it, till I let out
A long throng of impatient memories:
Together we mourned the way an instant dies.

There was a Frenchman too—some sort of pilot
In an ugly bandage. The three of us
Got talking all odd accents, and in a while it
Wasn't just words: we sang the Marseillaise,
The Land of Hope and Glory, and Auld Lang Syne:
Till on that note we reached a little town.

There we changed captors. We were back at base
With I-ties, or Italians, or plain Wops,
Who pinched our watches but could not refuse
To feed us on a diet of their slops.
And it was there that I first learned to sense
The tidy brutality of a barbed-wire fence.

It lay about us, rigorous as the proof
Of human ignorance finally seems to men—
—A limiting condition of all life,
Not just of ours—though it was we alone
Who acted camouflage halfways symbol to
It—and the laws we're hourly half-dragged through.

Everything worked by halves, and half-alive,
Half-starved and half-imprisoned as we were,
We were half-tempted almost to contrive
Escapes across that rusting wrestling wire;
But we did not. Instead, half-hearted jokes
Tried to persuade us it was all a hoax.

Then soon it ended, because we moved again,
This time on foot, and I don't really know
How many miles made up the phenomenon
That I describe, though not remembering, now.
Miles anyhow there were, no lack of them,
And afterwards more miles, and still the same.

It was the desert, and the sun was high
Or it went down; but it came up again;
A negroid Cyclops or at least his eye,
It pointed at us like an accusing gun
Which would go off if for a moment we
Forgot ourselves so much as to feel free.

Of course we had been guilty; so we went
On, though complaining, yet without arousing
Any emotion that was really meant.
We walked ahead, hypnotized by the horizon:
It wriggled in our sweat, in one round drop:
We did not reach it and we did not stop.

Then the night fell on us, whipping us with sand,
The cold, the dry grains in our nose and nails;
The tickling blankets and the loud command
To sleep or wake or empty filthy pails—
—Words in a language that meant no more to us
Than to a bird the fumbled blunderbuss.

We could not sleep, nor wake. We seemed to touch
A secret manifestation of the truth:
We lay down in the desert and learned to teach
Ignorance to professors: we learned to mouth
Old truths, and to forget them when they hurt,
Hurt us too much: truth became true as that.

We seemed like looking in a dead man's eyes
To see small stars dipped deep in the black pupil:
We'd suddenly and simply realize
How old astrologers could without scruple
Paste our lives on to them and advertise
Their rigmarole as wisdom to the wise.

For they were lying like in a black cup
Tealeaves made out of pure white light might lie
And formed a pattern; and a single drop
Brewed from those fragments of immensity
Could satiate thirst, it seemed, and let us pass
The ghost that most and momently haunts us.

What could have been the banquet of the gods,
I almost wondered, what could it have been
If these stars are the dregs? Are all men besides
Morsels to nibble when the feast is done?
I thought until the thought hardened past pain.
My thoughts grew eyes. They let the stars down in.

So for a long way: but it ended near
Tunis—you know the place? Most of us died
There—but you don't. You never will know where
Tunis pitted the map. It was outside
The squares they plant with pin-marks, beyond the four
Winds' quarters. I lived there. It is everywhere.

You'll reach it through a miserable month,
Sliding on sweat, cartwheeling over vomit,
Climb a few corpses and about the tenth
You'll turn about and think you've reached the summit.
That was your own one, was it? Not at all.
Here is another. You let your foot fall.

Daylight became a sticky mess of flies,
A filthy porridge stewing in our blood,
Lumpy with bubbles, and the rest of us
An ulcer, an excrescence, where they stood
Next me, a second; then they disappeared
And left me as before, and I despaired.

Starvation hits you innerwards like that,
Forces pattern on thought, on feeling, and all
We most think moral in man. It doesn't act
Only. It's something bigger: it thinks. And call
Yourself what you like, the image of God, the True,
Starvation alters reflection. It alters you.

And takes you down with it, through horrid slopes,
Along with shapes, and higher in your brain
It walks and wants, and everywhere escapes
Into its proper hunger, making the mind din
Over—mere mechanisms built to try
New methods out, try, try to satisfy.

Starvation can lead you to Tunis—the one I know.
It is an old town. There men have lived
Since men have lived, and those who died there knew
That it could hold their bodies, and believed
Others would find a burial ground there too.
I lived there, all of me. Don't go. Don't go.

The stench, the itch, the dysentery, the hours,
And then the moment when the guards brought bread:
I took the lot and gobbled on all fours
And didn't tell them that my mates were dead
Till the thick smell of them and the discoloured face
Made it impossible and I ate still less.

Four men, a breakfast roll, a pail of water,
With at the bottom suds of macaroni,
At least a dozen but about as bitter
As the green slime that rots across a penny.
Hell has its comforts. Those who died forgot
At least the worst of it but I can not.

For life goes on. It keeps on going, going
Over the old hard ground, and the unbroken
Heart breaks again. I felt my life-blood slowing.
Death was at work; when suddenly I was taken,
A slab upon a stretcher, to a ship.
I did not eat there and I could not sleep.

Guns snored from Malta. Planes bounced above my head
The decks and port-holes splashed into the water.
Winds swarmed and hopes subsided. Thoughts went
   dead;
And hours went pounding hard and helplessly,
Like iron pistons, into emptiness.
Then the sea loosened. We had come across.

And so they tended us, gave us to eat
From wholesome plates. We lived in an old castle,
And gradually our limbs at least forgot
They had been hungry. Lips began to whistle,
Fingers to hold a pen, and pain to go.
Thoughts bustled through us, hopefully to and fro.

It didn't last, of course, but nothing does,
And we enjoyed it, knowing it would end.
A train ran weekly and took some of us
Out of it somewhere but I couldn't find
A clue to the direction till one day
I was among the ones who went away.

It must have been two months between the two
Modes of starvation—one, the quick acute
And killing primary need I had come to know.
Death gurgled near it. . . . It seemed a mere brute
Rampant and miserable, plunging with a moan
Its whole weight at me; in me like a bone.

The other—but it was in Germany—
A perilous pedestrian sense of God—
It lasted longer, outlasting sun and snow
Two winters and three summers. I watched the slow plod
Of overladen feet, till I had seen
Footprints like letters form an articulate line.

Or rather—but we lived in a tin hut
With one of those long reaches for a prison
Where the slack landscape folding out of sight
Seems to crop up again behind the horizon;
At least we slept there, when we had got through
With hacking coal for sixteen hours a day.

They kept us there for coal, alive enough
To cut it in the dark, but not to think.
They gave us porridge and a kind of dough
Half-baked bread, and sticky soup to drink.
I ate it, gave them coal, two years and more,
And shivered in a blanket on a floor.

Any conditions continued long enough
Will stretch themselves until a man can live
All of him, in them; and the lowest life
Give highest impulse headroom, though he have
A hutch, a hole, a hill, to habit, and
Squalor alone to love and understand.

That is what baffles tyrants. Only death
Can end man's freedom to be all man can.
Prisons are perches. I went underneath
Then came up with a precious undertone
That swirled to song out of the damp dark
Through coughs that came with it and made it stark.

There were enough of them—incarnadined
The shining rock-face with thick frothy spittle,
And hours enough after the coal was mined
To watch how others bended or turned brittle,
Broke in a moment, and the hysteric calm
After the black barred ambulance had come.

Yet in the tunnel, at the rock-face, when,
Accumulated by exhaustion, thoughts
Would form and fold and hold themselves close in
About the point of peace, were other states.
The shift, twelve hours had gone, and six more yet.
The pick-axe slithered in my hand like sweat.

Huge blocks and boulders mined off hours ago
Would seem a sick weight, and my stomach turned
Into a sob, and memories of snow
And footprints tapering backwards through it burned,
Like tiny monosyllables blaze, with fear.
My weak arms worked. I seemed to disappear.

Lying along my belly, the rock roof
Two feet above, the wet rock floor upon
My muscles sliding, I seemed to grow aloof
From my own body or to grow a skin,
Flesh, form, and senses, deep within my own
And to retire to live in them alone.

My hands against the coal would grow transparent,
Then, like a match felt softly by its flame,
My arms would char into a wandering current;
Warm radiance crept up them till the same
Vivid transparence flooded every part
And I could see the beating of my heart.

As sedentary worms that burrow in
A froth of sand cement it with a slime
Out of their own skin, I too shed my shine
On to the rock below me till in time
It took the same transparence as myself:
I saw its seed, its kernel, through the filth.

And then above, the rock like catching fire
Bled into clearness to the pointed grass
That bled beyond it; and the sun that higher
Winds in its web this planetary mass
Grew clear; stars stood above it, and ranged behind
Its brightness like the working of a mind.

I saw the moments and the seasons swim
Precisely through me and I saw them show
Huts, hills and homes, and distance, and my dream
Of little footsteps shrieking in the snow
As they tip into darkness, all grow bright
And smother everything in transparent light.

I watched. A tender clarity became
That moment mine, as clear as through a hand
Bones shadow out into a candle's flame
And tender-terrible as to understand
Faults that the finding of has often killed
Pity and pain in you, fault-ridden child.

And I acknowledged. O I don't know what,
But greater grace than my acknowledgement
Could ever reach the edge of, or forget—
—A tender clarity that would not relent
Till I saw mercy from the merciless brink
Of thoughts which no mind born was born to think:

A tender clarity that is not understood
But by the helpless in a dangerous instant,
A perilous deity. O my good God,
Come quietly at last, and become constant.
The years grow small about me. I despair.
Impose your order on my every hour.

It was an order, yes! but not imposed
Though not within itself complete, and not
Abstract—an order, movement, force, composed
Of situations, things, which one great thought
Transparented completely through its mind:
Dawn; the long images lay down behind.

I was at mercy of them, am unable
Ever to meet except set in dismay
No, no, not shadows—but the implacable
Splendour descending, splitting tenderly
Skin, skull, and atom, till, though merely man,
I recognize a reason for all pain.

I saw the world, the world in full transparence,
Stark peaks through earth like vultures crowding down,
Become a symbol for its own appearance,
A system that completely and unknown
Was worked through by old forces and old laws
Which let it mean them, being what it was.

No other certainly. It didn't change
But stayed as still as in the stifled heart
Feelings not spoken, words would disarrange,
Can lie in hiding for their counterpart.
It was the world. Confuse no heaven nor hell.
The boring bubbling world you know so well.

The cold unclean and comfortable world,
Hard as an anvil, pointed, and as flat;
Circular saw, the orbit, square sphere swirled
Through bones, through brains; the spotted speedy spate
Of rivers, riders, racing with a will
Past men and mountains through the inexplicable.

Lying along my belly in the mine,
Or labouring footprints in the German snow,
I, the involved one, learned to love again
And, loving it, attempted to reach through
To the broad air, the people, though for years
My pit-prop prison peopled unawares.

I learned to love the self-same world as now:
For love of it, though its tranparency
Was my captivity, I planned carefully how
To reach through to it and in it to be free.
I killed a man. I killed him and escaped
Into it living. Then, at last, I wept.

I got away through the Bohemian South
And into Yugoslavia where I joined
A band of partisans who lived next to death.
In that excitement, thinking was postponed
Or sharpened hard on the best way to kill.
I kept myself alive, and that was all.

But now as years pass and the war is done
I find myself of evenings often enchanted
And guessing what goes on within my brain,
Conceive myself as of being haunted
By corpses more alive than his own flesh:
They dog me with a brittle tenderness

That breaks upon a whim, but nothing breaks
Through my continual sense of loss and sense
Of being cut off by simple slight mistakes,
Everyday errors, from an innocence
That is still mine though it lives a life apart
Folded transparently in the transparent heart.

MILTON

MILTON, his face set fair for Paradise,
And knowing that he and Paradise were lost
In separate desolation, bravely crossed
Into his second night and paid his price.

There towards the end he to the dark tower came,
Set square in the gate, a mass of blackened stone
Crowned with vermilion fiends like streamers blown
From a great funnel filled with roaring flame.

Shut in his darkness, these he could not see,
But heard the steely clamour known too well
On Saturday nights in every street in Hell.
Where, past the devilish din, could Paradise be?

A footstep more, and his unblinded eyes
Saw far and near the fields of Paradise.

THE PLANETS

UNDER the rings and green of syrup-water
the great pond fish in pewter, darkly weaving,
flutter their waving twilight. But to the watcher
warm in another nature, living the sun,
no creature, none, stirs in those coiled abysses;
and where those feathered nooses run, no dreamer
guesses the man, the summer, or his maker.

Now lean above and play the manna-maker:
here where the willows chequer skylit water,
scatter your bread. The lurker and the dreamer
loom their cold glitter to the warmer sun;
swimmer by swimmer, one by one, come weaving
up from the laving of their spun abysses—
great heaving fish lift faces towards the watcher.

Fierce in appalling blue there stands the Watcher,
fire of our nurture, shining-weather-maker,
walker in awful stature of abysses.
All those pale gases' weaker light the Sun
disperses with his own, as his the water:
those outer mysteries burn, invisibly weaving,
brighter by his removing from the dreamer.

Sunless infinity will drown the dreamer
though, by the glimmer of the stars, the watcher
nightly—the stitcher of that dimmer weaving,
by night believing in a future sun—
calls it the crown of loving of our Maker:
darker than fish in their strange town of water,
day-bitter stars flicker in blind abysses.

Out of the poet's pardons and abysses
the verses rise like fish; around the dreamer
the glamour of wild spaces rolls like water:
fact will not flatter—the armour of the sun
breaks down; there is no quarter for the watcher.
Though richer by his wane, with sun the makar
—searcher of meeker stars—heddles their weaving.

Poems and stars and fish, all darkly weaving,
sieving the mystery of their proud abysses,
go roving—secret races—till the makar
undresses, for the waker in the sun,
beauties that shun the talker and the dreamer:
the lying moon is for the rhymer, the watcher
of selves that shimmer on a pitcher of water.

For mystery is the poem's night and water:
daughter of truth, clad in the spectral weaving
of her begetter our cold-earth-wiving Watcher,
she—marcher about that unforgiving Sun
whose archer-beams we enthrone in wheeled
    abysses—
wears unknown light's embraces, until the dreamer
ceases to murmur against stars or maker.

XVIII

THE TREE ON THE PLAIN

THERE was the tree on the plain. It rose up
   Against the air, against the sky;
It defied God.
Its branches were like roots in the air; who could say
From which of those two it sucked its life,
The earth or the sky?

In the tree's roots worms curled; birds sang
In the green branches.
About its head
Clouds like white rocks sailed. Like black clouds
Bruising the roots, hindering worms,
Rocks settled.

There was the tree on the plain. It defied
God, who made it, earth that sustained it,
Me who observed it.
The sap, drawn from two roots, of earth and air
Sang in the trunk; the green leaves
Were bursts of song.

The plain under the tree, the sky above it,
The air around it.
They were like servants.
They pandered to its whims, were subservient to its
    beauty.
As for me, was I not proved
By its existence?

There is no tree on the plain. Or is it that I
No longer am?
Is there a tree on the plain
And not I?
Does the tree take root in the earth
Or take root in the sky?

THE ANIMALS

CUTTING the different shapes of bush,
He chances suddenly on the animal form:
Each shrub becomes a dog, a cat, a tiger.

Yet he does not stop to think as he crops
That in grief of leaf and branch they lack
The adequate life, that their roots
Bind them too sadly to possessive earth.

So he sleeps as the day declines, does not see
Their shadows yearn and lengthen,
And wistful, stretch in desire to be gone,
Away from the ordered garden, on legs
That cannot carry them, in living game.

And they grow as paradoxes, to be seen
Alive but still, sly, abject, posturing,
On the unmoving lawn—unchanged until
Their outlines fade with the growth of summer's
    green.

BIRKETT'S EAGLE

ADAM BIRKETT took his gun
    And climbed from Wasdale Head;
He swore he could spare no more lambs
    To keep an eagle fed.

So Birkett went along the Trod
    That climbs by Gavel Neese,
Till on his right stood Gavel Crag,
    And leftward fell the screes.

The mist whirled up from Ennerdale,
    And Gavel Crag grew dim,
And from the rocks on Birkett's right
    The eagle spoke to him.

'What ails you, Adam Birkett,
    That you have climbed so far
To make an end of Lucifer,
    That was the Morning Star?

'If there's a heaven, Birkett,
    There's certainly a hell;
And he who would kill Lucifer
    Destroys himself as well.'

The mist whirled off from Gavel Crag,
    And swept towards Beck Head,
And Adam Birkett took his aim
    And shot the eagle dead.

He looked down into Ennerdale
  To where its body fell,
And at his back stood Gavel Crag,
  And at his feet lay Hell.

Birkett scrambled off the rocks,
  And back onto the Trod,
And on his right lay Ennerdale,
  And on his left stood God.

'What was it, Adam Birkett,
  That fell onto the scree?
For I feared it might be Lucifer,
  That once was dear to me.

'And from Carlisle to Ravenglass,
  From Shap to St. Bees Head,
There's nobody worth vanquishing
  If Lucifer is dead.'

Birkett's dogs leapt all about
  As he came down the scree,
But he said 'I have killed Lucifer,
  And what is left for me?'

Birkett's lambs leapt all about
  As he came off the fell,
But he said 'I have killed Lucifer,
  And I am dead as well.'

But Lucifer the Morning Star
  Walked thoughtfully away
From the screes beyond the Gavel
  Where the eagle's body lay.

And as he went by Black Sail Pass
  And round below Kirk Fell,
He looked like young Tom Ritson
  Who knew the Birketts well.

And he came down to Wasdale Head,
    Young Ritson to the life,
With an apple in his pocket
    Which he gave to Birkett's wife.

THE HOARDING

IN the little room on the road I sat,
looking out at a cardboard eye
and a paper hat, that and a message
ten feet high. 'If you don't wear me
you will surely die.'

Tall in the window, she and I
counted the lanes in the heaving sky,
avoiding the stare of the cardboard eye
and the fear of the message ten feet high.

But she suddenly said, and her face was flat:
'I could never stand that, to spend my years
in a paper hat, under the beam
of a cardboard eye. I would rather die.'
And she jumped from the window, thirty years high.

Down below in the ageless tracks
I saw my lover white as wax
and I did not cry, but pulled the blinds
on the paper hat and the cardboard eye
leaving a message ten feet high.
'You will surely die.'

XXII

MY HAT

MOTHER said if I wore this hat
I should be certain to get off with the right sort of
  chap.
Well, look where I am now, on a desert island
With so far as I can see no one at all on hand.
I know what has happened, though I suppose Mother
  wouldn't see,
This hat, being so strong, has completely run away with me.
I had the feeling it was beginning to happen the moment I
  put it on,
What a moment that was as I rose up, I rose up like a flying
  swan,
As strong as a swan too; why, see how far my hat has flown
  me away,
It took us a night to come and then a night and a day,
And all the time the swan wing in my hat waved beautifully;
Ah, I thought, how this hat becomes me.
First the sea was dark but then it was pale blue
And still the wing beat and we flew and we flew
A night and a day and a night and by the old right way
Between the sun and the moon we flew until morning day.
It is always early morning here on this peculiar island,
The green grass grows into the sea on the dipping land.
Am I glad I am here? Yes, well, I am,
It's nice to be rid of Father, Mother and the young man.
There's just one thought causes me a twinge of pain—
If I take my hat off, shall I find myself home again?
So in this early morning land I always wear my hat,
Go home, you see—well, I wouldn't take a risk like that.

XXIII

THE LITERARY SWAN

HAVE others noticed the effect, or am I the only one,
On our poets, ancient and modern, of the sight of a
swan?
It is almost impossible to pick up a tome
Of the work of one of our major poets without finding a pome
About a swan; whilst the young moderns, who write those
slender volumes of verse
About despair in grim cities, still centres, joyless copulation
and so forth, in a style habitually astringent and terse,
Are even worse.
There is something about a swan which, if it does not bring
out the poet in every man,
At least loosens the buttons of every poet in a way that
nothing else can.
At sight of a swan all the long-haired lads and short-haired
lasses
Reach for pen and paper and sit on their tidy asses
To write lyrics so different from their usual constipated style
and theme
That they sometimes go to the other extreme.
Thus we get innumerable pomes about white swans, black
swans, living swans, dead swans,
Still swans, moving swans, starving swans, fed swans.
And if you and I, who probably regard the swan as a photo-
genic but unremarkable bird,
Should find it strange that it is so often the subject of emo-
tional ditties on the Third
Programme and in the loftier weeklies, perhaps we ought to
remember that the swan has always been a literary fowl,
Much more so, for instance, than the raven and the owl,

Which rarely appear in print in modern times,
And never got any higher, anyway, than Gothic novels and
    nursery rhymes.
But the swan, to the fevered and nimble
Mind of a poet has always been essentially a profound symbol
Of something or other, while its neck, arched in the shape of
    a query,
Inevitably reminds the wretched serious writer of his weary
And endless search after ultimate truth, a theme he can never
    shirk,
And which turns every country walk, because of swans, into
    a job of work.
Then again, all poets from time to time feel that they need a
Subject free of the restraints of society, so they naturally
    write about Leda
And the swan, and find the perfect escape
From convention in a wallow of classical rape,
Though it is true that most people still prefer to read
    the modern and unmythological accounts of such
    capers
In the Sunday papers.
Nor will it have escaped the notice of anyone who is *à la*
    recherche de la raison d'être
Du cygne littéraire, or even of any intelligent *homme de
    lettres,*
That a very considerable swan once went to roost,
Heavily disguised as a sensitive hero, in the pages and pages
    of Proust.
But the main reason for the popularity of the swan with the
    ungregarious herd
Of poets is probably that it is such a dignified and delicate
    bird
(Except on land, but even then some poets' metres reproduce
    with devotion
Their subject's ungainly, clumsy, waddling, flat-footed
    motion).
You never hear a swan make the walls of solemnity crack
With a quack,

Or see it rooting about arse-end up in primeval muck
Like a duck.
Which is really why I should like our poets to cease making
such a fuss
Of the swan, and write about something else for a change,
the puffin, for instance, or the plat-billed duckypuss.

XXIV

BALLAD OF THE FIVE CONTINENTS

IN blue Bristol city at tall-tide I wandered
  Down where the sea-masts their signals were shining,
  I heard a proud seaman on the poop-deck reclining
Shout to the stars that about the ship blundered
  On the high harbour lie six shifty daughters
  Their bodies are straight, their eyes are wide
  Here is the key of their burly bedchamber
I have unlocked it, I replied.

As I went down Water Street beneath the blond sun
  The trees of cold Christmas screaming with starlings
  Sweet screamed the birds as my delicate darlings
Scanned at my hand the black-buttered gun
  Think of the collar my bonny, my beauty
  Think of the hangman with hands so red
  Pray, pray that he does his duty
I am that hangman, I said.

As I walked in Wine Street the silk snow was falling
  And night in her Asian hair hung her comb,
  Soft sang the yellow-faced seaman of home
The gong and the coconut-fiddle recalling
  In the vermilion forest the dancer
  Adorns with gold thorns his holy head
  Will you not seize his hands, his fingers?
I am the dance, I said.

In Bread Street in summer we saw the boys hauling
   The Yankee-white wheat on the bowl of the bay,
   Between us the sword of the sun where we lay
Bloody with poppies, the warm sky our shawling
    Sly sing the sirens on the coast of California
    The oyster-fingered, the easy-eyed,
    Tiding their tune in the gin-wicked palaces
The song is mine, I cried.

Down by the dockside the green ships groaning
   Ten-roped writhe on the ragged sea,
   Blessed are they with the laurel tree
Now in the prow stands a saint for the stoning
    Sound the salt bell on the mound of the ocean
    Fish for a prayer in the pool of the dead
    When the storm strikes, speak the word on the waters
I am that word, I said.

XXV

CONVERSATION ON STACKPOLE HEAD

TIME, if we had a watch, would point to four.
　Against the light there wheeling over two score
Blackbacks peddle their reason mewing to the cliff.
Is it worth a guess, that crying, if
I know the bounds of life? Vary the game,
Demonstrate briefly that the lame
Emmet will always trundle in the hoppling last
Flax grain of the nine hestors, how fast
Soever the night falls. Excellent! Depend
On it that is no more than a net whose end
The floats mark yonder under cliff. Even half a man
Could stomach this without a cardigan.

No wind to speak of and the south-east roll
Flattening somewhat. If that hole
Goes past the immediate rabbit to the sea
This limestone headland and the lee
Cliff landward are fretted further by the tide
Than one would think. This side
Is dangerous. See the rocks boiling at the jut
Where the race is. A slip would gut
One soon enough, and the sea feeding round the toe
Step quietly up. Sun coming out, you say? No,
Not if I know it, not in a hundred years, not
In a lifetime. Even this anchusa has the spot,
Winded about the edge and sour. Without a watch
We loose an hour and make a shorter catch.

XXVI

THE SEWIN*

I FISHED the Seiont for a thousand years;
Up from the Halfpenny Bridge to Cwm-y-Glo
Those flagellated miles of water ran
The faster for my whip: the melted snow
Battered Caernarvon Castle like a storm.

I heard the fresh-run sewin leap along
The pools to Padarn and the high-hung redds
Beyond the lake; night after night they ran.
They thrust the stream to sea with tails and heads
Urged in from ocean by the weight of roe.

I sought my silver leaping love among
The midstream middeep lies of July noons
With a worm of doctrine from the Northern
    Schools,
Rolling a thunder by the feeding stones.—
The slim and vagrant shadow abode aloof.

I tantalized her with a delicate fly
And mended untold miles of morning line
Sailing my gauzy mirage past her nose,
An ephemeral dream of fantasy so fine
That only love could so disdain; and did.

I spun a minnow up, across, and down
Until the moon came up to look and laugh.
I changed my wheedling tactics then, and with
A whole millennium's unalterable lust
I got her with a maggot—and a gaff.

* *Sewin:* Sea-trout (Welsh).

XXVII

ACCIDIE

THE waterfall is empty now:
   Along the arid reaches
Of gullied rock, over the gravel beaches
At last exposed, only the warm air whispers
A memory of thunder.
Under that jagged wall
Where the dark salmon lunging
Once thrust against the plunging
Whiteness, up, over the lip of the fall,
And onward, like some legendary mortal
Set an impossible task by gods both jealous and stern,
Withers a trembling fern.

A man's dry mood may seize upon such pictures
To drain them of all meaning but his own:
He will not be the first
For whom an image of drought has briefly quenched
Intolerable thirst.

XXVIII

SEPTEMBER ON THE MOSSES

WAIT, tide, wait;
    Let the mosses slide
In runnels and counter-flow of rock-pool green,
Where web-foot mud-weeds preen
Leaves spread in the sunshine; where
On slow air-ripples the marsh aster lays
Innocuous snare of sea-anemone rays.

Wait, tide, wait;
Behind your wide-
as-winter ebb the poplars of the waves
Turn up their underleaves of grey.
Thunder-blue shadows boom across the bay.
But here the silt is green, the salt is bright,
And every grass-tongue licks its summerfull of
    light.

Autumnal tide,
Mauve as Michaelmas daisies, bide
Our while and summer's. Let the viscous sun
Percolate the turf. Let small becks run
Yellow for ever with shine, and the flood of
    this moment
Hold back time and shut the gate.
Wait, tide, wait.

Deciduous tide,
On the willow whips of inshore billows the
  inside
Edge is brown. Crying 'Never!'
Delays no due tomorrow,
And now is ever
By being not by lasting. So
With pride let this long-as-life hour go,
And flow, tide, flow.

XXIX

NO ANSWER

In the slow lapse of unrecorded afternoon,
When nothing seems to change but history itself
Unfolding at the pace of clouds or even weeds,
The window murmurs lightly to the vacant room,
And seems as if it commented with mild surprise
On some arrival, timely or unique;
Slow by the rapid stream, perhaps, or quick in the slow
    skies.

Why does the window murmur—and to whom?
What notable event does it report
That's far above the heads of furniture,
Nor heeded by the absent-minded room?

Is it first cuckoo-fall?—the double word
Falling like seed into the wood, instant with Spring?

Or is it rose-fall?—end of the first rose,
Spilled from the hand of Summer, pensively?

Perhaps first apple-fall?—scatter and thud,
And Autumn here that moment, cornucopia slanted?

Or is it only the first snow-fall?—one,
One, and then one, slid furtive down, as if
Winter himself had thought the moment haunted?

Windows look out of rooms at poetry,
That pours back through them, lyrical in birds,
Epic in weather, narrative in streams.
But they look only out, half-conscious of a being
Shadowed behind them, borrowing their eyes.

O little window, when you murmur, 'Do but look!'
Never ask who listens now. Never inquire
Why soundlessness should grow into a habit,
Helpless and final as the dust.
                                        Suppose
She may be resting yet in the great bed,
Tuned always to your accent, though her heart
Is listening miles away to mine.—Might she
Not lie so still? Never so long, so still?
Should there, long since, have come to you, at least,
The flicking over of a page—at least
Her busy pencil, whispering word by word
The letter she would send—at very least
A sigh?
                        So would she sigh,
In the dark ages of the afternoon,
When you would draw her to some poetry
(Fall of the word, the rose, the fruit, the fleeting
    crystal),

So would she sigh a war away—since tears,
If tears were let, would rain away the world:
Sigh in the great bed for its emptiness,
The waste of poetry, the waste of years.

XXX

THE RUNNER

I STOOD idle with a key in my hand,
And through the thickset hedge I saw a runner pass
Running slowly through the crisp Autumn.

Through the close hedge I saw his knees
Like pistons, and his head, the head of a man absorbed
In grave action, beautiful and restrained.

The red and white, flashing beyond the hedge,
And the runner passing up the hill, are gone,
While I stand idle with a key in my hand.

NOVEMBER SPRING

THIS twenty-ninth day of November
as I walked in dazed delight
my cheek was fondled by the amber

air, gentle as the hand of May;
and fingers of oak and elm invented
designs on a mother-of-pearl sky.

It was a marvellous, out-of-season
day: the children's cries were jets
of joy that mingled and showered in a dozen,

no, in a thousand drops of sound.
Bareheaded, coatless, boys raced reckless
on bicycles, wove swift ampersands,

exulting in the fearful thrill
of courting yet skirting in the nick
the inevitable crash and fall.

And briefly casting off weekday cares
menfolk observed the Sunday ritual
of hosing and polishing their cars

until in cellulose sheen and splendour
matched and mirrored with coloured truth
the shining clarity of the hour.

THE REPROOF

WHY should I mourn
  When a few lines of verse,
Accomplished with much toil,
Are scorned; or, worse,
Blandly ignored by those
Whom I would chiefly please:
With dark November here,
Why should I mourn for these?

Today I worked
With wheelbarrow and broom
In a grey solitude
Of misty gloom,
Brushing, bearing away
Towards their smouldering pyre
Leaves which already seemed
To have been flushed with fire.

I worked, and thought
How various, how fair
Were these insignia
Of the dwindling year—
More fair, I felt, more bright
Than ever they had been
Even in April's prime
When they were fresh and green.

Since art like this,
So far beyond my best,
By its creator's will
Thus runs to waste,
Why should my spirit now
With such resentment burn?
With dark November here
I do not dare to mourn.

XXXIII

ROMAN HYACINTH AND CHRISTMAS TREE

The Christmas flowers are shaped like conifers,
Of the dark tree the white obverse,
The tree is a night sky that underlies
And silvers its embroideries,
And only through its darkness shine so far
Spaced on its midnight branches moon and star.
There the light touches down in flight and takes
The sheen of webs and falls and flakes.

The silver hyacinth, though in its flower
It follows the tree's spread and spire,
Out of its time an essence has arisen
Of light, adorned by the dark season;
Wearing the shadowed air between its curled
Petals as human beauties wear the world;
Wearing our age of nightfall and black frost
Like sable ribbons at its breast.

The flowers are fresh as green, with green shadow
Touched, and the leaves as bright as snow;
And all this airy spike fines to an arrow
Whose path of light I cannot follow.
Flower of clear bells, plain in complexity,
Only earth's darkness paints your white for me.
Innocence lost, the long way must become
For men and worlds the shortest path to home.

THE SNOWMAN

Do not expect to find the first again,
Do not hope to close your fingers on the rain
Or see authentic sunshine falling on the sea.
Though you are sure you once went through
The seasons, snow to snow, do not go abroad again
In search of that first rain.

Be glad you have forgotten what the rain first told,
What the snow decided or the sun disclosed.
Rejoice that you continue lost to all you surely knew
Before you knew you-knew-it-lost.

Men and women go about, about they go,
Hands slipped or joined to catch that rain
Or cup that sunlight in the snow;
But ever swift the snowflake flies,
Cloud cumbers up the landscape of the face or hip,
Rain blurrs the speech of eyes,
Sun dries the lusting lip.

No lisp of love, no love of language will suffice
To shape those first soft syllables of ice;
No flush of glands, no gesture of the greedy hand
Will loose the symbols that the snow in falling loosed
    before
The snowman melted in the thaw.

XXXV

EARTHBORN

MY meditation puts into my hands
A manageable globe traced round with lands
Where I survey all action and all art.
    My eyes grow wide: I sit and think
    Of those whom talent sets apart,
    Of those who tread a crumbling brink
    Of danger, and of those whose speech
Best taught me to avoid the shifting sands,
The handsome, brave, and wise, I think of each.

Grateful that such a richness should have grown
Tangling from seeds that friends of mine have sown,
I know the surface fruits would have no worth
    Were there no value given by
    The vital middle of the earth,
    A warm and generous energy.
    Turning, I sink within at length,
Persephone like, past seams of gold and stone
To the plutonic darkness and the strength.

The doves have closed their tails above my head.
Lock my door, tell the callers I am dead.
And feeling round those subterranean walls
    About the hopeless cavern land
    Of drops and ends and waterfalls,
    I meet a warm familiar hand:
    Yours, yours, the hand for which I grope,
The hand that still to my right rule has led
And gives the earthborn unequivocal hope.

XXXVI

ANNIVERSARY

THIS fig tree spreads all hands towards the light,
    Five broad fingers to each, solid and still
  As those that are chiselled on pulpit or stall.
And yet the light pervades those carven leaves,
Not as my dark hands divert the sun
  If I hold them before my face—
  These invert it, let it pass,
A green effulgence that the trunk receives.

These fifteen years I have spread my hands to the light
    of your love.
Its rays should long ago have made me strong:
  Did my remorse for wrong,
Or fears filter its power from the light,
Or did my darkness divert it from my heart,
  That I am still so callow and unsure,
  And cannot think to endure
Even the shortest winter out of your sight?

XXXVII

THE PRICE

THE sword suspended by a hair
Above our feast, our tête-à-tête,
Has now fulfilled its threat.
Censorious neighbours everywhere
Would say that we deserved this fate,
And mock at our regret.

But the most dire conditions laid
Between us when the joy began
With mutual consent,
Forewarned us that the price we paid,
You the woman, I the man,
Were no impediment.

Secretly we gave and took,
Incredulous, yet thankful too
That furtive love could show
What canon law with bell and book
Gave not, because it never knew
Such charity might grow,

Such trust, endurance and delight,
Such riches from the meagre dish
That we were forced to share.
Therefore in this, our latest plight,
We can defy, as we would wish,
The sword, the severed hair.

XXXVIII

WESTMINSTER CHIMES

Black hat, black cane, striped leg man,
laconically elegant, cool as a fan.
I wonder if your love can ever be
as much to you as mine to me.

Ice in a furnace, silk-haired bird,
hopping on one leg, chirping a word,
no one lover could ever see
the soul in you that mine does in me.

Paper fingers, pen crutched ears,
cocktail shakers, ice in beers,
your arctic lover could never be
as true to you as mine to me.

He swung his eyes and he looked at me,
then he looked at my lover. Woe is me.

·

XXXIX

XXXVIII

COMMUNICATION

No use to speak, no good to tell you that
A love is worn away not by the one
Who leaves but by the one who stays and hopes,
Since you would rather have the hoping still
Than be yourself again. What can I say
Who know, better than you, the one who has
Moved on, away, not loving him at all?

And certainly to you I would relinquish
This knowledge held in other ways of feeling
Though dressed up in the properties of passion
Looked at by you. Something is deeply held
By me who never deeply searched at all
And we are not yet wise enough or subtle
To offer anyone a state of mind.

This the particular problem, and I search
A power over our general condition,
Where love is like a landscape we can change
And where desire may be transformed to friendship
If friendship gives the really wanted knowledge,
Where we can see the end and have the power
To take the journey there a different way,
And we can move our minds as we move houses:
Where love is more than lucky in the land.

BE STILL AWAY

And so you are returned.
And, yes, you are welcome again
For the talk and the qualified loveliness and
the burned-
Out passion you scattered and spent
Far from my long young pain.

And my bed is lightly lent
Just to remember your shape,
Just to renew in myself what you incisively
meant
In my distant heart of a maid
Before your casual escape.

If you had always stayed
We should not lie now so narrow
With nothing of hurt: the years of use would
have paid
In indifference at most
Not in this best. But tomorrow

Be still away as you used.
Stay young for me and lost.
The echo of my first love grows confused
And you a stranger
Hardly worth that cost.

XLI

THE TEMPEST

IT is the only story I can tell—
I lost my home and lover in a gale.
The house went over and the windows fell.

Is it a common thing? O wish me well!
Would that I were not drunk upon this tale.
It is the only story I can tell.

All night, all night, I hear those wind-clouds
  swell
That I innocent thought to be hail.
The house went over and the windows fell.

Tell me O fog was there a warning bell?
I keep repeating till my song is stale.
It is the only story I can tell.

Above the lightning's blast the devil's yell;
Then at that moment all my love went pale:
The house went over and the windows fell.

Of love and lover there is left the shell,
And I demented pass by town and vale.
It is the only story I can tell,
The house went over and the windows fell.

DIALOGUE

'TELL us again of love and death,
　Opposed, that we may picture both
Who cannot think them separate.
Death a mere empty frame we hate
And only love
At one remove:
So giddied by the turning wheel,
We need a mirror, loss, to see the loved
　　one whole.'

'Never again, since she
First breathing on the mirror hid
The macrocosmic mystery,
To leave us lost; till newly centred, grown
More partial, we should need
No other loss to prove
The wholeness of our love,
Nor any quickening discord but our
　　own.'

XLIII

THE RECONCILIATION

After our trial,
  Accusation and denial,
Evidence on oath
And cross-examination, both
Speaking together or with black silence seeking
To condemn, to justify, more than by speaking,—
After all this we find ourselves at large,
Have nothing to defend, prefer no charge.

And after our disease
Which made us sweat, stare, pant for breath
And shewed quite clearly the old age which is
Latent in faces, and the masks of death—
For indeed we had the look of those too deeply
  and dangerously ill to weep—
After all this we are better, and can see
The unhoped-for daylight of recovery.

We find now what was proved by word
Of twisted mouth baseless, absurd,
And the clear and unforgivable offences
Of no more weight than any sick-room fancies.
We find our arms not made for threats and vaunts
And lips not just for labial consonants,
And the same faces over which were shed
Such alien lights, are recognized instead,
Friends out of danger, darlings from the dead.

CHURCH CLOCK WINDING

So the men, the ancient men,
The men with curiously-cut clothes,
Were this small! Small as this doorway in the arch
Leading to steps cut like an apple-core
From the rubble upthrust of the tower.
Forty-three triangular steps go upward
To the clock chamber. Forty-three to that room.
Then upward still another rock-hewn flight
To the iron-tongued, silent, listless bells,
Holding long echoes of forgotten sound.

So the men, the ancient men
Toiled forty-three steps upward with their clock,
A huge, black jangling of wheels and cogs,
Steel ropes and one great pendulum,
A cyclops eye, swinging eternally.
But then, in the hands of the ancient men,
It did not swing, but came the upward forty-three
A round black lump of impassivity.
Some blacksmith made it in a village forge,
Calculating the length of swing to mark an hour
Or second, made these adept wheels and cogs
Which creep at snail's pace, every move
A sundial's shade; while like an ogre's teeth
The iron weights drop from the tower's top,
Steal through the day and night, the night and
    day
A little downwards past the bells. That journey
Takes till Tuesday night from Sunday.

Past the pendulum and clock in wooden shed
Until, by Wednesday night, they grind the dust
Of the room below the clock where once
The ancient men stood in a circle,
Bell-ropes in their hands. You see their names
Cut in the lancet windows at the time
Of Waterloo, Trafalgar and the Nile,
Or even at the century's turn.

But the men, the ancient men who have no names,
Who brought here the clock to mark the hours
Of their own and others' lives and deaths,
Where are they now? Some drunken
Graveyard stone may mark their night
Beneath the timepiece which they reared
Above their skeletons and left to me
That circular, upward forty-three,
And gave to me the task which they begun.
For he who first put down his hand and swung
That pendulum, created by his act a special Time
In which were clearly stated, logically, exact,
His figure and my own, Time's servitors.
Had he but held his hand beyond that moment
Both of us were free.
But having done this act he gave his freedom,
Mine as well, into the hands of what he had created.

His clock outlives him, Time has made *him* free
But not so I who toil that forty-three.

AFTER READING A BOOK ON FERNS
for John Betjeman

SAY Tabitha lived here with her ferns,
off the High Street, in a cul-de-sac
into which heavy lorries would back,
darkening her raftered room, filling it
with echoing oaths too strange to shock
lonely Tabitha living with her ferns:
> adiantum cuneatum gracillimum
> nephrolepis exaltata hillsii
> phyllitis scolopendrium crispum.

The sword-fern cascading from the stand
(her kittens would toy with it until
she tapped them), the hart's-tongue on the sill,
sturdiest of all, the mist-maidenhair
on the what-not, tremulous and still,
were ferns to her; to those who understand:
> nephrolepis exaltata hillsii
> phyllitis scolopendrium crispum
> adiantum cuneatum gracillimum.

Say that she found a most subtle joy
in her green world. Quite ignorant of
the sublimations of luckless love,
she lightly dusted them with her breath,
marvelling how their fronded beauty throve,
having no need of Latin to enjoy
> phyllitis scolopendrium crispum
> adiantum cuneatum gracillimum
> nephrolepis exaltata hillsii.

When they laid Tabitha in the ground,
within sound of matins and evensong,
they planted over her the hart's-tongue
               (phyllitis scolopendrium crispum)
for its hardness; but the tender ferns
they heartlessly left to perish among
the garbage of a cat-infested ground
               (nephrolepis exaltata hillsii
                adiantum cuneatum gracillimum).

This, I fear, is a dark universe
for the luckless heart, the tender plant;
but it would be the most godless cant
to refuse to give thanks for the things
that have consoled us for a vain want.
Tabitha, help me to praise in my verse
                adiantum cuneatum gracillimum
                nephrolepis exaltata hillsii
                phyllitis scolopendrium crispum.

WOOD PIGEONS AT RAHENY

ONE simple and effective rhyme
Over and over in the April light;
And a touch of the old time
In the serving-man, stooping, aproned tight,
At the end of the dappled avenue
To the easy phrase, 'tereu-tereu,'
Mulled over by the sleepy dove—
This was the poem I had to write.

White wall where the creepers climb
Year after year on the sunny side;
And a touch of the old time
In the sandalled Capuchin's silent stride
Over the shadows and through the clear
Cushion-soft wooing of the ear
From two meadows away, by the dove—
This was the poem that was denied.

For whether it was the friar's crime,
His leanness suddenly out of tune;
Or a touch of the old time
In the given phrase, with its unsought boon
Of a lax autumnal atmosphere,
Seemed quaint and out of keeping here,
I do not know. I know the dove
Outsang me down the afternoon.

XLVII

CITY PIGEONS

HEAVY the opal rose-green tame
Pigeons, that seem, for all their flame's
Encumbered flickering, as bound
Stem-linked as flowers to the green ground,

Or sessile in the city's mown
Precincts as grave or building stone.
Heavy they rise when feet fall near them
And strange it seems that space will bear them,

And strange that flight is their condition
Like men who own pride and ambition—
These kin to lilac flower falls
And stones that form the roots of walls.

THE DOVE AND THE TREE

Night after empty night
I wait for the dove to descend
To its heart in the dark tree,
Fluttering wing and breast
(Wind-tremulous at flight's end)
Folded to slow rest
Under the leaves of love
And plain fruit's simplicity.

Diffident, urban, small,
The anchored garden lies
Chained to blind-flying night
And its passionate uncertainties.
Uneasy behind its wall
Of crumbling, local stone
The lawn waits for the light.
The bird is above, alone.

Now sap in the bubbling wood,
Stung into sudden fire,
Illuminates each leaf
And vein of the tree's desire.
Spun to a tumbling flood
Incendiary leaves leap high
And make of their own belief
A beacon for the sky.

The strumming summer trembles
Towards its ripe perfection
Among the purple grasses
And as each second passes
It gains a brief reflection
Thrown from the fiery tree
In phoenix ecstasy;
And the heavy darkness crumbles.

Alone in the plumed air
Flies the plummeting, blind dove.
Alive through its harsh despair
The tree is alight with love—
The resinous tall flames
Their noisy pillars send
Into the ruffling clouds.
When will the dove descend?

When shall the bird descend
To her home in the landlocked tree?
I have no means to end
The intolerable tragedy,
But watch, aloof and sad,
Caught in its own distress,
Beyond my wall their world
Dissolve in emptiness.

'WE GO TO THIS . . .'

WE go to this as connoisseurs to girls
    For pleasures in the ripening form,
And should these high phrases not suffice,
The sap not run in thinking them,
Should these bedizened thoughts not stir
We are as strained and fractious as these lechers are.

The seeming syllables of the water-stones
And fiery verbiage of the winds,
Our lust for finding words to phrase
A speaking likeness of such things,
If we should fail at all in this
We are as stale and tedious as the lecher is.

God ordered the green earth to spin
And made the sun and moon to shine
So that by day or night it shows
His care and constant discipline,
Then ringed it round with winking stars to be
The flashing mirror of reality,

Or so 'Timaeus' says. The words suffice
To raise up images of a darker truth
Not our concern, the leching soul desires
Never to wrestle with profundities,
Only the chiming phrases are enough to stir
Such creatures as we curious lechers are.

It is not virtue or the truth invites
These explorations of the word
Made flesh, but the true music of the phrase,
Its singing centre which delights,
That we are firm in this
Makes us impenitent as the lecher is.

L

A TEACHER OF THE DEAF
(for C.E.)

Her purpose is to mould words for them, wholly
Out of the ordinary sight of things, make meanings
To link and connect with objects, to effect communication.
And from their silent country they stretch out
Their wordless thought to her indicating lips, they grasp
Aspects of movement in her face, and make them
Symbols for things themselves, in their feeling sense.

An object is the easiest. Think of *cat*,
The living animal, that is, and moves;
(*Is*, of course, is a difficult word; existence
Is no simple attribute.) Yet, incidentally,
Think can be, surprisingly, quite quickly taught.
Thinking, somehow, can be told, or shown, or mimed—
A hand at the head, an expression, then an action.

But only slowly come the classes of things—
So easily confused with the things themselves.
Three cats will not mean *animal* in kind, but only *cats*.
And numbers, though they grasp them, do not help here;
They do not define, but merely multiply *cat*.
Or adjectives will be mistaken for what they describe:
Black cat seems *cat*, a *heavy* book—just *book*.

Yet these are the foothills of her mountain.
On steeper slopes come *for* and *to* and *the*,
Articles, and prepositions of place. These are confused
With the actions done in teaching them. For example,
I walk to the door: walk and *door* are easily learnt,
But *to* and *the* slip by. Her patient lips
Convey a movement, but no meaning stirs.

Some means must be found and used, by way of signs,
To create the elusive sense of such expressions,
That the climbers might move on from the seen and
   known, and
Up to the strange, invisible *idea*. She will have to make actions
Seem to possess a meaning beyond the facts
And subtler than the movement. She will have to come
At last to the hardest in the range of word and thought,

The unseen abstract, content of mind alone.
This is an escarpment for her. What is *real*? *Unreal*?
Or what is *wise*? Or *foolish*? *Good*? Or *bad*?
But once beyond that, the mountain can be viewed
From its highest point; and her sense can be comprehended.
She has now to begin to point out the extended land,
For they, with this summit reached, can *understand*.

MONOLOGUE OF A DEAF MAN

Et lui comprit trop bien, n'ayant pas entendu.—Tristan Corbière

It is a good plan, and began with childhood
As my fortune discovered, only to hear
How much it is necessary to have said.
Oh silence, independent of a stopped ear,
You observe birds, flying, sing with wings instead.

Then do you console yourself? You are consoled
If you are, as all are. So easy a youth
Still unconcerned with the concern of a world
Where, masked and legible, a moment of truth
Manifests what, gagged, a verb should have told,

Is observer of vanity and courage
And of these mirror as well; that is something
More than a sound of violin to assuage
What the human being most dies of: boredom
Which makes hedgebirds clamour in their blackthorn
     cage.

But did the brushless fox die of eloquence?
No, but talked himself, it seems, into a tale.
The injury, dominated, is an asset:
It is there for domination, that is all.
Else what must faith do deserted by mountains?

Talk to me then, you who have so much to say,
Spectator of the human conversation,
Reader of tongues, examiner of the eye,
And detective of clues in every action,
What could a voice, if you heard it, signify?

The tone speaks less than a twitch and a grimace.
People make to depart, do not say 'Goodbye.'
Decision, indecision, drawn on every face
As if they spoke. But what do they really say?
You are not spared, neither, the banalities.

In whatever condition, whole, blind, dumb,
Onelegged or leprous, the human being is,
I affirm the human condition is the same,
The heart half broken in ashes and in lies,
But sustained by the immensity of the divine.

Thus I too must praise out of a quiet ear
The great creation to which I owe I am
My grief and my love. O hear me if I cry
Among the din of birds deaf to their acclaim,
Involved like them in the not unhearing air.

REASONS FOR ATTENDANCE

THE trumpet's voice, loud and authoritative,
Draws me a moment to the lighted glass
To watch the dancers—all under twenty-five—
Shifting intently, face to flushed face,
Solemnly on the beat of happiness.

—Or so I fancy, sensing the smoke and sweat,
The wonderful feel of girls. Why be out here?
But then, why be in there? Sex, yes, but what
Is sex? Surely, to think the lion's share
Of happiness is found by couples—sheer

Inaccuracy, as far as I'm concerned.
What calls me is that lifted, rough-tongued bell
(Art, if you like) whose individual sound
Insists I too am individual.
It speaks; I hear; others may hear as well,

But not for me, nor I for them; and so
With happiness. Therefore I stay outside,
Believing this; and they maul to and fro,
Believing that; and both are satisfied,
If no one has misjudged himself. Or lied.

LIII

ENGLISH FILM

IT was one of those modest comedies, calculated
To raise a reluctant titter in the savage breast
       that hated England—
About a humble tom-fool making good; some four or
  more
Young girls, quite fetching though quite fully dressed;
       a villain who didn't really mean
To be, whose guns turned into children's playthings;
Some views of London streets in sunshine, with those
       buses so peculiarly clean—
It twitched discreetly at the world's strained heart-strings.

Outside a ragged wind is blowing off the Yodo River:
Along the tidy consulates the flags are jerking,
Sick for home. Thinner than ever,
The nimble women furl themselves in their kimonos,
As twilight thickens into yellow, yellow with the dusty
Dead of an over-peopled country, thick with the lurking
Solicitings of a country too rich in girls.
       Yet we walk in our inner weather—
Unsolicited and sudden, the memory of kindness
  uncalculated,
In some half-dozen lands, unrelated by blood or colour,
Unimpelled by gods or goods. Is there really no room
       to live together—
This side the cinema, this side the windswept tomb?

LAKE GARDA

In memoriam H. S. L.

MORNING was mist on this great sweep of water,
morning was breezes, steepening sun,
deepening blue of lake, the cypresses
sheer in the great heat, the cobbled lane
climbing intently on:
climbing among the silver olive-sprays,
oak, fig and vine,
the laurel's depth and soft acacia's flutter.

Morning was Sirmione, clear and far
over the lake; ranged peaks of stone,
long inlet spread in light, their changing colours
strengthened in this transfusion of sun
spreading through every vein,
moving through slow fields and slanting valleys
in grape and grain,
in the swept grasses and the cypress-tower.

Morning in spangled trees, in sudden autumn
of grape and blackberry on the tongue,
sweet, but distilling so much memory
of beauty lost, so swift and fierce the pang
that all the morning hung
in trembling filaments a hand might play—
if string and string
could sound the interval of separation.

Arching to play, the hand could find no key:
morning was silence, the strings numb.
How slowly now one learns, the dead being gone,
to read again: treasuring in the palm
the clear flat golden form
of fallen olive-leaf, praising the clean
blue heaven of calm
called butterfly, this twinkling pinch of sky.

Alphabet only: night will come
long before words can bring the meanings home.

PEACE IN THE WELSH HILLS

CALM is the landscape when the storm has passed,
Brighter the fields, and fresh with fallen rain.
Where gales beat out new colour from the hills
Rivers fly faster, and upon their banks
Birds preen their wings, and irises revive.
Not so the cities burnt alive with fire
Of man's destruction: when the smoke is spent,
No phoenix rises from the ruined walls.

I ponder now the grief of many rooms.
Was it a dream, that age, when fingers found
A satisfaction sleeping in dumb stone,
When walls were built responding to the touch
In whose high gables, in the lengthening days,
Martins would nest? Though crops, though lives,
    would fail,
Though friends dispersed, unchanged the walls
    would stay,
And still those wings return to build in spring.

Here, where the earth is green, where heaven is
    true
Opening the windows, touched with earliest dawn,
In the first frost of cool September days,
Chrysanthemum weather, presaging great birth,
Who in his heart could murmur or complain:
'The light we look for is not in this land'?
That light is present, and that distant time
Is always here, continually redeemed.

99

There is a city we must build with joy
Exactly where the fallen city sleeps.
There is one road through village, town and field,
On whose robust foundation Chaucer dreamed
A ride could wed the opposites in man.
There proud walls may endure, and low walls feed
The imagination if they have a vine
Or shadowy barn made rich with gathered corn.

Great mansions fear from their surrounding trees
The invasion of a wintry desolation
Filling their rooms with leaves. And cottages
Bring the sky down as flickering candles do,
Leaning on their own shadows. I have seen
Vases and polished brass reflect black windows
And draw the ceiling down to their vibrations,
Thick, deep, and white-washed, like a bank of
    snow.

To live entwined in pastoral loveliness
May rest the eyes, throw pictures on the mind,
But most we need a metaphor of stone
Such as those painters had whose mountain-cities
Cast long, low shadows on the Umbrian hills.
There, in some courtyard on the cobbled stone,
A fountain plays, and through a cherub's mouth
Ages are linked by water in the sunlight.

All of good faith that fountain may recall,
Woman, musician, boy, or else a scholar
Reading a Latin book. They seem distinct,
And yet are one, because tranquillity
Affirms the Judgment. So, in these Welsh hills,
I marvel, waking from a dream of stone,
That such a peace surrounds me, while the city
For which all long has never yet been built.

A SENSE OF HISTORY

WALKING at random over the mountainous moor-
      land
With cry of curlew and wild mare's warning neigh
Held in an unhedged wind enough to knock your head
  off,
At the bitter end of a swept and solitary day

I came at last to the shores of an incongruous water
Perched without purpose upon a mountain summit.
The eastern end was a shelving bank of stone
And the terrible wind blew stiff waves upon it.

And, head down along the edge, I could not help notice
How all the long perimeter was similarly guarded
With single slices of stone, each patiently placed
Against the waves' water and into a crude mosaic.

Who dry-walled these shores? What men had planned
These back-breaking banks and lived on the low
Secure island? (It is there still, and still the stone
Ungainly circles that were houses how long ago.)

I only know that I was suddenly kneeling—
While over me flew the torn, unheeding froth—
And plugging with scales of stone the wave-worn gaps,
Ten frozen fingers against the loud storm's tooth.

Then, heading homeward through the embracing marsh-
  land,
I faithfully found with quick and unearned skill
The hidden paths that led to the acquired valley,
Quite dry and hidden, away from wind, lake, hill.

NORTHERN NOCTURNAL

HEAVEN rises massive with its stars over
Hekla, Quinag, the smoke and cloud, the gloom
Naked in Striven, the glade of deer, of human
Crofts the half-lost glen and dereliction.
North the glacier, north the broch; and the voices
Struggling from boat and peat and granite street.
The worlds pace in their thickets, Cassiopeia
Studs with faintest crystal the Pole's crust.
The blue and crawling floe stiffens in the cold,
The dolphin glides with brow of ice. Glasgow
Stands like a mailed tomb where the full flood of bronze
Palls the million of the living in strong and perdurable folds.

Winter and midnight! It is a still beauty.
I whisper, and the frosty steeples prickle.
One great word might speak this city awake.
How many hopes buried in its cradling stone,
Atom by atom with girder, glass and gable
Retain their cries, and when the heart recalls them
Cry out again, from their vision buried in vain!
Treasures of things made everlasting, joys
Liker fire than light, shouting and phoenix daysprings
Breaking the lagging calm of common years—
How could life bear so much desire! Meagre and mute
In its youth seemed life, yet life devoured desire. Moonlight

Is silvering the stark Necropolis,
The pavement glitters like a river, space
Is turned to time. Back, back! Where are your ghosts
O miseries, and O anxieties

Show me those unappeased, your ancestors!
The silent tenements breathe deep. Night moves.
No brick, no grave, no gutter lies so silent
As the gaunt arteries and walls of the heart
Immense in its desertion, a dead city
Inert and icy, defiant, whole and solitary.
Hidden it lies like a great diamond, and only this haunting
December hour of stars evokes its ghostly glancing.

Who walks its flashing roads? Who laughs and sings?
Who turns the corner of time? This face I know,
Those outstretched arms, the smile—sun, moon, wind,
  friends
Cling, plucking the flying rags, cry
Remain and remember, blow with their lips to fires
Extinguished, till the love leaps up in pain
From sleep to speech through flame. Black lay the bridge
Above its drowned lamp-images; it shakes:
A late train blazes and shrieks past. I watch
As its train of sparks rides off into the darkness
Among the freezing stars, and over the Clyde's dark streams
Falls through those trembling wakened struts of wintry steel.

When all is dark indeed: the whirl, the luminance
Clouded from identity, the glimmer on slate and cobble
Faded, and the wan flash of windows gone,
The streetlamp and the Plough; when all is quiet
As dust in dead waves on the Sea of Showers,
As tranquil and as noiseless as those years
The voyaging universal radiance divides;
When all is cold as cavern-flume, sea-floor,
Jupiter, or Pluto in the Thule of the sun:
And then to blackness, silence, cold, my sense
Chokes blind in breaking death, death like this night will free
My fire and shower of desire to the stone and the steel and the
    sea.

GLASGOW 1960

RETURNING to Glasgow after a long exile
Nothing seemed to me to have changed its style.
Buses and trams all labelled 'To Ibrox'
Swung past packed tight as they'd hold with folks.
Football match, I concluded, but just to make sure
I asked; and the man looked at me fell dour,
Then said, 'Where in God's name are you frae, sir?
It'll be a record gate, but the cause o' the stir
Is a debate on "la loi de l'effort converti"
Between Professor MacFadyen and a Spanish pairty.'
I gasped. The newsboys came running along.
'Special! Turkish Poet's Abstruse New Song.
Scottish Authors' Opinions'—and, holy snakes,
I saw the edition sell like hot cakes.

LIX

THE WASTE SCOTLAND

With apologies to Sc*tt G*ds*r M*cd*rm*d and of course to Mr. Eliot

THE warrld is a scroggie croft o unco drouth
Wi blastit learnin and wi donsie men
Whan will we see the wet of Clyde oorslap
And plenish the ramfeezl'd howes agen?

April's the reuchest month, ryvin the mools
It gars the gawans brak oot o the knowe
And whar's the deed mon that you derned awa
Has he begun to braird, or has he no?

There is not even Lallans on the braes
But stour and skriegh o sassenachs and rats
And birkies playing chess or tossin cabers
And warlocks making glamorie wi the cartes.

D'ye ken the tummlin toûrs o unreal touns
Vienna, Auchtermuchty and Dunblane?
Lenin, thou pluckst me burning from the reik:
The cock skirls from the dowlie kirk: Amen.

KINGS

You send an image hurrying out of doors
  When you depose a king and seize his throne:
You exile symbols when you take by force.

And even if you say the power's your own,
That you are your own hero, your own king
You will not wear the meaning of the crown.

The power a ruler has is how men bring
Their thoughts to bear upon him, how their minds
Construct the grandeur from the simple thing.

And kings prevented from their proper ends
Make a deep lack in men's imagining;
Heroes are nothing without worshipping,

Will not diminish into lovers, friends.

NEXT STOP PERTH

THAT was my place that I am far from.
Those were my hills I climbed all over.
Through that tunnel I went under
My now over-passing railway line.

That was my love I burned for the touch of.
That was my faith I worked and lived for.
In those dreams was pained foreknowledge
Of the chilling age-years that now are mine.

Those were my ghosts that I gave way to:
Now from within the shape of terror
I see me young and in frozen fear of
My fetch that is giving the countersign.

IF THE POOR MAY SPEAK

IT is hard having poverty
always at elbow, a too intimate friend:
the crust left over at the thin day's end
must be put aside carefully,

for tomorrow has ambitions
beyond our knowing, and possibly will come
over the threshold with severer and more glum
looks, not to say intentions,

than now; so let us honour
whatever we are able not to spend,
for this being miserly's a way to lend
another day its colour—

if it's mere charity
diet on which the daybreak falls too clear,
simply to continue with the light is dear,
surviving what is niggardly:

which always comes to winter
too frequently with us, drab holiday
guest we don't want, so we can never say
the worst weather's over.

The world is savage and terrible,
we know, and live as if it were not so
and waking wore a different light tomorrow,
in whose eye a fable

of coins and food in plenty
and permanent summer hanging from the sky,
was common and real, and all else a lie,
the begging bowl never empty.

A VOICE IN THE VOID

i

A VOICE called, and I heard,
And hearing, I replied:
It was no wandering bird
But a human voice that cried;
A lost voice in the night—
And do lost voices lie?
I took my self for light
And answered, Here am I.

ii

There was no world as yet,
No world, no way, no choice,
Only, in silence met,
Voice calling unto voice:
But with that clear response
My eye could dimly see,
And where was darkness once
A world began to be.

iii

A face was turned to mine:
A face or but a mask?
I could not then divine
This question I should ask.
The eyes of clearest gray,
The brows of shady black.
I did not turn away
But steadily looked back.

iv

I saw the pupil bright,
The iris flecked and grained
With grains and flecks of light;
But as my vision strained
To comprehend the face
It lost composure, and
Those flecks of light gave place
To grains of swirling sand.

v

I saw, as still I gazed,
Those eyes so clear and bright
Were but a film that glazed
The silence of the night;
Each grain of desert sand
Rose up and spread afar,
Far off each took its stand
And was a glinting star:

vi

A glinting star that might,
A wandering, frenzied spark,
Evade the scope of sight
And lose itself in dark
Had I an instant failed
Or faltered in intent
Vision to keep unveiled
And every covering rent.

vii

O terror! to be there
In silence absolute;
In vacuous spaces where,
Immeasurable, mute,

Could be no word, no world,
No answering voice begin,
And every silence whirled
Back on its origin!

viii

All words would be denied
Should that denial stand,
All worlds away subside
To lose themselves in sand
Backwards—the very void
Engulf itself again,
With every seer destroyed
And every vision vain.

ix

Though void the night and vast,
And though each flittering light,
Its limit overpassed,
Seeks to forsake the sight;
Transfixed, as if a Cross
Were stretched athwart the sky
To mark the total loss
Of possibility:

x

I know I must endure
In silence deep as death,
To hold my vision clear
And, all alone, keep faith
That in the trembling dark
Each wandering star draw nigh,
And every grain and spark
Be focused in an eye.

XLIV

THE NEW AGE

SHALL I tell you the signs of a New Age coming?
It is a sound of drubbing and sobbing
Of people crying, We are old, we are old,
And the sun is going down and becoming cold,
Oh sinful and sad and the last of our kind
If we turn to God now, do you think He will mind?
Then they fall on their knees and begin to whine
That the state of Art itself presages decline
As if Art has anything or ever had
To do with civilisation whether good or bad.
Art is wild as a cat and quite separate from civilisation
But that is another matter
That is not now under consideration.
Oh these people are fools with their sighing and sinning
Why should Man be at an end, he is hardly beginning,
This New Age will slip in under cover of their cries
And be upon them before they have opened their eyes.
Well, say geological time is a one-foot rule
Then Man has only been here about half an inch to play the
  fool
Or be wise if he likes, as he often has been,
Oh heavens how these crying people spoil the beautiful
  geological scene.

Index of Titles and Authors

I	How to Fill in a Crossword Puzzle	Vernon Scannell	9
II	Illusion	J. D. Lawson	11
III	The House where I was Born	C. Day Lewis	12
IV	The Carpenter	Clifford Dyment	14
V	Jesus and His Mother	Thom Gunn	16
VI	Adopted Child	Brian A. Rowley	18
VII	The Shape of a Bird	Laurence Whistler	19
VIII	A Burial	Sydney Tremayne	21
IX	At Lengthening Range	Laurence Whistler	22
X	Orpheus	Thomas Blackburn	24
XI	Mme. Emilie Teste	George Rostrevor Hamilton	25
XII	The Tall Man	Alexander Henderson	26
XIII	The Wrong Road	C. Day Lewis	28
XIV	By Heart	Richard Drain	30
XV	The Transparent Prisoner	Burns Singer	31
XVI	Milton	Edwin Muir	43
XVII	The Planets	Terence Tiller	44
XVIII	The Tree on the Plain	John Smith	46
XIX	The Animals	Alan Brownjohn	48
XX	Birkett's Eagle	Dorothy S. Howard	49
XXI	The Hoarding	Norman Harvey	52
XXII	My Hat	Stevie Smith	53
XXIII	The Literary Swan	Cyril Hughes	54
XXIV	Ballad of the Five Continents	Charles Causley	57
XXV	Conversation on Stackpole Head	Roland Mathias	59
XXVI	The Sewin	W. H. Canaway	60
XXVII	Accidie	Peter Dunn	61
XXVIII	September on the Mosses	Norman Nicholson	62

XXIX	No Answer	_Laurence Whistler_	64
XXX	The Runner	_Margaret Webb_	66
XXXI	November Spring	_Fallon Webb_	67
XXXII	The Reproof	_Ralph Lawrence_	68
XXXIII	Roman Hyacinth and Christmas Tree	_E. J. Scovell_	70
XXXIV	The Snowman	_Gabriel Fielding_	71
XXXV	Earthborn	_Thom Gunn_	72
XXXVI	Anniversary	_Anne Ridler_	73
XXXVII	The Price	_Richard Church_	74
XXXVIII	Westminster Chimes	_Norman Harvey_	75
XXXIX	Communication	_Elizabeth Jennings_	76
XL	Be Still Away	_Catherine Lyons_	77
XLI	The Tempest	_Emily Coleman_	78
XLII	Dialogue	_Michael Hamburger_	79
XLIII	The Reconciliation	_Hal Summers_	80
XLIV	Church Clock Winding	_James Turner_	81
XLV	After Reading a Book on Ferns	_F. Pratt Green_	83
XLVI	Wood Pigeons at Raheny	_Donald Davie_	85
XLVII	City Pigeons	_E. J. Scovell_	86
XLVIII	The Dove and the Tree	_Leslie Norris_	87
XLIX	'We go to this . . .'	_H. S. Eveling_	89
L	A Teacher of the Deaf	_Alan Brownjohn_	91
LI	Monologue of a Deaf Man	_David Wright_	93
LII	Reasons for Attendance	_Philip Larkin_	95
LIII	English Film	_D. J. Enright_	96
LIV	Lake Garda	_Christopher Lee_	97
LV	Peace in the Welsh Hills	_Vernon Watkins_	98
LVI	A Sense of History	_Leslie Norris_	101
LVII	Northern Nocturnal	_Edwin Morgan_	103
LVIII	Glasgow 1960	_Hugh MacDiarmid_	105
LIX	The Waste Scotland	_Hubert Nicholson_	106
LX	Kings	_Elizabeth Jennings_	107
LXI	Next Stop Perth	_Naomi Mitchison_	108
LXII	If the Poor May Speak	_Kenneth Gee_	109
LXIII	A Voice in the Void	_D. S. Savage_	111
LXIV	The New Age	_Stevie Smith_	114

The Contributors

(The numerals at the end of each biography indicate the number and page number respectively of the poet's contribution.)

THOMAS BLACKBURN. Born 1916 in Cumberland. Educated at Bromsgrove School and Durham University, and now teaches English at Marylebone Grammar School. He is married to a painter. Publications: *The Outer Darkness* and *The Holy Stone* (poems). [X, 24].

ALAN BROWNJOHN. Born 1931 in London. Educated at Brockley County School and Merton College, Oxford. At Oxford founded and edited small literary magazine, *Departure*. Publications: poems in *World Review*, *Truth*, etc., and a pamphlet *Travellers Alone* [XIX, 48; L, 91].

W. H. CANAWAY. Born 1925 in Cheshire. Educated at Altrincham Grammar School and University College, Bangor. Now working as Technical College Lecturer. Writes pseudonymously on fishing [XXVI, 60].

CHARLES CAUSLEY. Born 1917 at Launceston. Served in the Royal Navy 1945–1946. In 1954 was elected a Bard of Cornwall (Bardic title 'Morvarth' *Poet of the Sea*), and was also awarded a Travelling Scholarship of £100 by the Society of Authors. Publications: *Farewell, Aggie Weston* and *Survivor's Leave*, poems. Also *Hands to Dance*, short stories [XXIV, 57].

RICHARD CHURCH. Born 1893. He published his first book of verse in 1917. At first a civil servant and colleague of Humbert Wolfe, he has for the last twenty years been a free-lance writer and a literary adviser, with some forty books to his name, including *Collected Poems* published in 1948 [XXXVII, 74].

EMILY COLEMAN. Born 1899 in Oakland, California, now living in Rye, Sussex. Her first poems were published in *Transition* in Paris. Publications include *The Shutter of Snow* and *Melville on the Land* [XLI, 78].

DONALD DAVIE. Born 1922 in Barnsley. Educated at Barnsley Grammar School and St. Catharine's College, Cambridge. Fellow of Trinity College, Dublin, and lecturer in English in Dublin University. Publications: *Purity of Diction in English Verse* and *Brides of Reason*, poems [XLVI, 85].

RICHARD DRAIN. Born 1932 at Wimbledon. Educated at Latymer Upper School, Hammersmith, now reading for a degree in English at Sidney Sussex, Cambridge. His poems have been published in *The New Statesman*, *The Spectator* and *The London Magazine* [XIV, 30].

PETER DUNN. Born 1918 at Brighton. Educated at Varndean Grammar School. He is a schoolmaster, and his poems have appeared in *John O'London's Weekly* and *Poetry Review* [XXVII, 61].

CLIFFORD DYMENT. Born 1914 in the Midlands. Educated at Loughborough Grammar School, and has worked as a documentary film director. He received an Atlantic Award in 1951. Publications: *Poems 1935–1948*; *Experiences and Places*, poems; and *Cecil Day Lewis*, critical essay for the British Council [IV, 14].

D. J. ENRIGHT. Born 1920 in Leamington Spa. Educated at Downing College, Cambridge. He was once lecturer in English at the Farouk I University, Alexandria, and Organizing Tutor (for Black Country) in the Extra-Mural Department of Birmingham University. Now teaches English at Konan University, near Kobi, Japan. Publications include *A Commentary on Goethe's Faust*, *Season Ticket*, *The Laughing Hyena and Other Poems*, and *Academic Year* (novel) [LIII, 96].

H. S. EVELING. Born 1925 in Newcastle-upon-Tyne. Studied English at King's College, Durham University. Was awarded the Earl Grey Fellowship. For the past year has been doing post-graduate work in philosophy at Oxford. Publications: several poems in Oxford magazines and in *Grub St.* [XLIX, 89].

GABRIEL FIELDING. This is the pseudonym of a doctor at present living in Kent. Born 1916 in Northumberland, he was educated at St. Edward's, Oxford, Trinity College, Dublin, and St. George's Hospital. Publications include *The Frog Prince and other Poems*, and *Brotherly Love*, novel. He is writing a second book of poems, and a trilogy to supplement *Brotherly Love* [XXXIV, 71].

KENNETH GEE. Born 1908 in London. He is married. His poems have appeared in *Horizon*, *The Listener*, *Poetry: London*, *Poetry Quarterly* and other magazines. He is now painting as well as writing. Publications: *The Dead Can't Hurt You*, short stories, and *32 Poems* [LXII, 109].

THOM GUNN. Born 1929 at Gravesend. Educated at Trinity College, Cambridge, and St. John's College, Cambridge. Also Stanford University, California. Editor of *Poetry from Cambridge*. Author of *Fighting Terms*, a collection of poems [V, 16; XXXV, 72].

MICHAEL HAMBURGER. Born 1924. Educated at Westminster School and Christ Church, Oxford. He has published two collections of verse and several of translations, the most recent of which is *Holderlin: Poems*. He was one of the editors of *New Poems: 1953* [XLII, 79].

GEORGE ROSTREVOR HAMILTON. Born 1888 in London. Educated at Bradfield and Exeter College, Oxford. He was Presiding Special Commissioner of Income Tax 1950–53 and was knighted in 1951. He has published many books including *The Inner Room*, *The Carved Stone* and *The Russian Sister*, poems; and *The Tell-tale Article*, criticism [XI, 25].

NORMAN HARVEY. Born 1921 in Bristol, and is a teacher of mathematics at the Bristol Junior Technical School. Has published poems in *Zebra*, the West Country magazine [XXI, 52; XXXVIII, 75].

ALEXANDER HENDERSON. Born 1910. His published works include *Aldous Huxley*, *Eyewitness in Czechoslovakia*, and two novels, *Freedom's Crooked Scar* and *The Dangerous World*. His poems have been published in *Orion*, *Poetry Quarterly*, *The Windmill* and *The Listener* [XII, 26].

DOROTHY S. HOWARD. Born 1921 at Sheffield. She has contributed to *Punch* and other periodicals [XX, 49].

CYRIL HUGHES. Born 1920 at Liverpool. Educated at Liverpool Collegiate School, Bangor Normal College, and the University of Paris. Now teaches English and History. Several articles, stories and poems published [XXIII, 54].

ELIZABETH JENNINGS. Born 1926 in Lincolnshire. Her first book of poems was published in 1953 and was awarded an Arts Council Prize. Poems published in *The London Magazine*, *Encounter*, *The Listener*, *New Statesman and Nation*, *The Spectator*, *The Times Literary Supplement*, *Botteghe Oscure* and *The New Yorker* [XXXIX, 76; LX, 107].

PHILIP LARKIN. Born 1922. Publications include *The North Ship*, poems, and *A Girl in Winter*, novel [LII, 95].

RALPH LAWRENCE. Born 1899 at Bangalore, S. India. Educated at the City of London School. Publications: *The Millstream and other Poems*, and a prose impression of Surrey in the *Vision of England* series. He has also contributed an essay to *Essays and Studies* [XXXII, 68].

J. D. LAWSON. Born 1922 at Manchester. Educated at Manchester Central High School and the University of Manchester, where he obtained an Honours Degree in Geology. This poem is his first published work [II, 11].

CHRISTOPHER LEE. Born 1913. Educated at Latymer Upper School and Merton College, Oxford. He has held French and Italian awards for the study of art history. Since 1946 he has been an extra-mural lecturer for Cambridge University. Has published four books of verse, including *Under the Sun* [LIV, 97].

C. DAY LEWIS. Born 1904, in Ireland. Educated at Sherborne School and Wadham College, Oxford. Now Professor of Poetry in the University of Oxford. Publications include *The Poetic Image*, verse translations of Virgil's *Georgics* and *Aeneid* and a number of volumes of verse now collected in *Collected Poems, 1954* [III, 12; XIII, 28].

CATHERINE LYONS. Born 1922 at Gainsborough. Educated at Doncaster High School and Birmingham University, where she edited *The Mermaid*, the University Magazine. Has taught at schools in Birmingham and Epsom [XL, 77].

HUGH MACDIARMID. This is the pseudonym of Christopher Murray Grieve, born 1892 in Dumfriesshire. Publications include *Sangschaw*, *Penny Wheep*, *A Drunk Man Looks at the Thistle*, *The Islands of Scotland* and *The Golden Treasury of Scottish Poetry* [LVIII, 105].

ROLAND MATHIAS. Born 1915 in Wales. Educated at Caterham School and Jesus College, Oxford. For the last six years he has been Headmaster of the Grammar School, Pembroke Dock. Publications: *Break in Harvest* and *The Roses of Tretower*, both volumes of poems [XXV, 59].

NAOMI MITCHISON. Born 1897 at Edinburgh, and brought up partly in Oxford and partly in Scotland. Has worked on a farm, served on the local Council, and been interested in politics. Publications include *The Conquered*, *The Corn King and the Spring Queen*, *The Blood of the Martyrs*, *The Bull Calves* and *Travel Light* [LXI, 108].

EDWIN MORGAN. Born 1920 at Glasgow, He is a lecturer in English at Glasgow University. Publications: *The Vision of Cathkin Braes*, poems, and *Beowulf*, a translation into modern English verse [LVII, 103].

EDWIN MUIR. Born 1887 in Orkney, where he lived until the age of fourteen, when his family moved to Glasgow. Worked for a number of years as a clerk in various commercial firms. Later he became a journalist, translator and author, and travelled widely in Europe. After the last war he was Director of the British Institute in Prague and later in Rome. Most recent of his many publications in poetry and prose are *Collected Poems* in 1952 and *An Autobiography* in 1954 [XVI, 43].

HUBERT NICHOLSON. Born 1908 in Hull. He is a sub-editor at Reuters, is married and lives at Epsom. His published works include *Here where the World is Quiet*, *Half My Days and Nights*, *A Voyage to Wonderland*, *Little Heyday* and *The Mirage in the South* (poems) [LIX, 106].

NORMAN NICHOLSON. Born 1914 at Millom, where he still lives. Publications: *Five Rivers*, *Rock Face*, *The Pot Geranium*, all works of verse. He has also published two verse plays, *The Old Man of the Mountains* and *Prophesy to the Wind* [XXVIII, 62].

LESLIE NORRIS. Born 1920 in Merthyr Tydfil, and is now a schoolmaster at Bath. Poems have appeared in *Poetry (London)*, *The Welsh Review*, *Wales*, *Little Reviews Anthology*, *Bugle Blast*, *New Poems: 1954* and have been broadcast [XLVIII, 87; LVI, 101].

F. PRATT GREEN. Born 1903 in Liverpool. Educated at Rydal School, Colwyn Bay. His poems have appeared in *Time and Tide*, *Outposts*, *English*, *The Poetry Review*, etc. Publications include *This Unlikely Earth*, poems [XLV, 83].

ANNE RIDLER. Born 1912, and is the mother of four children. As Anne Bradby she edited a volume of Shakespeare criticism in the World's Classics series, and has also edited *A Little Book of Modern Verse* and the new edition of *The Faber Book of Modern Verse*. She is the author of several books of poems and verse plays, among which is a collection of poems called *The Golden Bird* [XXXVI, 73].

BRIAN A. ROWLEY. Born 1923, in Lancashire. Educated at Bolton School and Corpus Christi College, Cambridge. Now Lecturer in German at University College, London. Poems have appeared in *Poetry from Cambridge in Wartime*, *Poetry from Cambridge 1947–1950*, and in various periodicals [VI, 18].

D. S. SAVAGE. Born 1917. In 1938 he was awarded the Jeannette Sewell Davis Prize for a group of poems. Publications include *The Autumn World, Don Quixote and other Poems, A Time to Mourn* and *The Withered Branch* [LXIII, 111].

VERNON SCANNELL. Born 1922. Has broadcast several times on the Home and Overseas Services, and some of his poems have been broadcast on the Third Programme. Has published two novels, *The Wound and the Scar* and *The Fight*, and one book of poetry, *Graves and Resurrections* [I, 9].

E. J. SCOVELL. Born 1907 in Sheffield. Two collections of her poems have been published, *Shadows of Chrysanthemums* and *The Midsummer Meadow*. A number of her poems has been broadcast and published in various periodicals [XXXIII, 70; XLVII, 86].

BURNS SINGER. Born 1928 in New York City, though a British national. He has contributed poems to *Botteghe Oscure, The Times Literary Supplement, Encounter*, etc. [XV, 31].

JOHN SMITH. Born 1924 at High Wycombe, he is the Director of a Literary Agency. Has published three volumes of poetry, *Gates of Beauty and Death, The Dark Side of Love* and *The Birth of Venus* [XVIII, 46].

STEVIE SMITH. Born in Hull. She has worked in a publisher's office. Publications include *Novel on Yellow Paper, Over the Frontier, The Holiday* (novels); also *A Good Time Was Had by All, Tender Only to One, Mother, What is Man?* and *Harold's Leap* (poems) [XXII, 53; LXIV, 114].

HAL SUMMERS. Born 1911 in Yorkshire, and now lives in Kent. Publications: *Smoke After Flame, Hinterland,* and *Visions of Time* [XLIII, 80].

TERENCE TILLER. Born 1916 in Cornwall. Since 1946 he has worked in the B.B.C. Features Department as Writer-Producer. He was awarded the Chancellor's Medal for English Verse at Cambridge in 1936. He has published three books of verse: *Poems, The Inward Animal* and *Unarm, Eros* [XVII, 44].

SYDNEY TREMAYNE. Born 1912 in Ayr. Educated at Ayr Academy. He has been a journalist since he was seventeen, and is now leader writer for a national newspaper. Publications: *Time and the Wind, The Hardest Freedom. The Rock and the Bird* is about to appear [VIII, 21].

JAMES TURNER. Born 1909, in Kent. Publications: *Mass of Death*, *My Life with Borley Rectory*, *Rivers of East Anglia*, *Murder at Landred Hall*, *A Death by the Sea*, *Pastoral*, *The Alien Wood* and *The Hollow Vale* [XLIV, 81].

VERNON WATKINS. Born 1906 in Maesteg, Wales, and now lives on the Gower peninsula. He has contributed poetry and translations of French and German poetry to various periodicals and anthologies here and in America. Publications: *The Ballad of the Mari Lwyd and Other Poems*, *The Lamp and the Veil*, *The Lady with the Unicorn*, *The Death Bell*, *Selected Poems* and *The North Sea* translations from Heine) [LV, 98].

FALLON WEBB. Born 1899 in Tunisia, and educated at Taunton School. He is a retired insurance auditor. Has contributed a few poems to literary periodicals [XXXI, 67].

MARGARET WEBB. Born 1911 in Maidenhead. Educated first in Ceylon and then in Westmorland. Married, with four children. This is her first published poem [XXX, 66].

LAURENCE WHISTLER. Born 1912 in Kent. Educated at Stowe and Balliol College, Oxford, and is a writer on architecture. Publications include *The World's Room* (poems), *Sir John Vanbrugh, Architect and Dramatist*, and *The English Festivals* [VII, 19; IX, 22; XXIX, 64].

DAVID WRIGHT. Born 1920 in Johannesburg. Educated at Northampton School for the Deaf, and at Oxford. He received an Atlantic Award in 1950. His second collection of poems, *Moral Stories*, was published last year, and he co-edited with John Heath-Stubbs *The Faber Book of Twentieth Century Verse*, and an anthology of 19th century poetry, *The Forsaken Garden* [LI, 93].